The
Beagle

An Owner's Guide To

A HAPPY HEALTHY PET

Howell Book House

Hungry Minds, Inc.
Best-Selling Books • Digital Downloads • e-Books • Answer Networks
e-Newsletters • Branded Web Sites • e-Learning
New York, NY • Cleveland, OH • Indianapolis, IN

Howell Book House
Hungry Minds, Inc.
909 Third Avenue
New York, NY 10022
www.hungryminds.com

For general information on Hungry Minds books in the U.S., please call our Consumer
Customer Service department at 800-762-2974. In Canada, please call (800) 667-1115.
For reseller information, including discounts and premium sales, please call our
Reseller Customer Service department at 800-434-3422.

Library of Congress Cataloging-in-Publication Data
Roth, Richard.
The beagle: an owner's guide to happy, healthy pet/by Richard Roth.
p.cm.
Includes bibliographical references
ISBN 0-87605-389-4
1. Beagles (Dogs) as pets. I. Title. II. Series.
SF429.B3R68 1995, 2001   95-41273
636.7'53—dc20   CIP

Manufactured in the United States of America

20 19 18 17 16 15 14 13 12 11

Series Director: Kira Sexton
Book Design: Michele Laseau
Cover Design: Michael Freeland
Photography Editor: Richard Fox
Illustration: Jeff Yesh
Photography:
    Front and back cover photos supplied by Paulette Braun/Pets by Paulette
    Courtesy of the American Kennel Club: 14
    Joan Balzarini: 96
    Mary Bloom: 19, 25, 28, 36–37, 80, 96, 136, 145
    Paulette Braun/Pets by Paulette: 2–3, 5, 45, 46, 49, 57, 60, 63, 75, 96
    Buckinghamhill American Cocker Spaniels: 148
    Sian Cox: 134
    Dr. Ian Dunbar: 98, 101, 103, 111, 116–117, 122, 123, 127
    Dan Lyons: 96
    Scott McKiernan: 7, 8, 9, 23, 44, 56, 62, 94
    Cathy Merrithew: 129
    Liz Palika: 133
    Janice Raines: 132
    Susan Rezy: 96–97
    Richard Roth: 12, 20, 27, 53
    Judith Strom: 11, 21, 29, 31, 32, 38, 40, 41, 42, 55, 58, 66, 96, 107, 110, 128, 130,
    135, 137, 139, 140, 144, 149, 150
    Kerrin Winter & Dale Churchill: 96–97
Page creation by: Hungry Minds Indianapolis Production Department

Contents

part one

Welcome to the World of the Beagle

1 What Is a Beagle? 5

2 The Beagle's Ancestry 14

3 The World According to the Beagle 25

part two

Living with a Beagle

4 Bringing Your Beagle Home 38

5 Feeding Your Beagle 46

6 Grooming Your Beagle 55

7 Keeping Your Beagle Healthy 63

part three

Enjoying Your Dog

8 Basic Training 98
by Ian Dunbar, Ph.D., MRCVS

9 Getting Active with Your Dog 128
by Bardi McLennan

10 Your Dog and Your Family 136
by Bardi McLennan

11 Your Dog and Your Community 144
by Bardi McLennan

part four

Beyond the Basics

12 Recommended Reading 151

13 Resources 155

Welcome
to the
World
of the

part one

Beagle

External Features of the Beagle

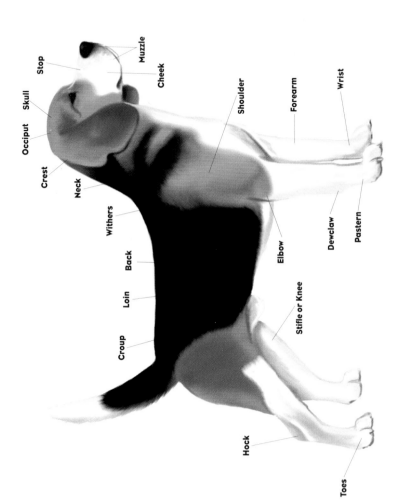

chapter 1

What
Is a
Beagle?

Introduction to the Beagle

A Beagle, contrary to public belief, is not a dog. The Beagle is a *hound*, a member of a select fraternity within the canine world, bred for centuries to hunt as part of a large pack. He is the little cousin of the

Foxhound so often depicted in the numerous paintings of horses and hounds in the English countryside. He is the more active, less melancholic cousin of the Basset Hound, and, like the Basset, his primary quarry is the hare or rabbit.

The little puppy asleep on your lap may not know all this, but it is important for *you* to know this, because it will help you better understand this marvelous little creature—how he thinks, why he does some of the things he does, and why he has been "designed" to look the way he does. And the more you know about your little hound and his "kin," the better you will be at meeting his needs and keeping him happy during what should be a long and positive relationship.

Breeding to a Standard

As with any recognized breed—be it cows, horses or canines—there is a "standard of perfection" that describes what the Beagle should look like. You would do well to read it over a few times, comparing the "word pictures" with the illustration in the front of this book. This will give you a feel for the breed "type"—that which sets the Beagle apart from other breeds.

WHAT IS A BREED STANDARD?

A breed standard—a detailed description of an individual breed—is meant to portray the *ideal* specimen of that breed. This includes ideal structure, temperament, gait, type—all aspects of the dog. Because the standard describes an ideal specimen, it isn't based on any particular dog. It is a concept against which judges compare actual dogs and breeders strive to produce dogs. At a dog show, the dog that wins is the one that comes closest, in the judge's opinion, to the standard for its breed. Breed standards are written by the breed parent clubs, the national organizations formed to oversee the well-being of the breed. They are voted on and approved by the members of the parent clubs.

While the standard is used by show judges to select the best hound in a show class, it should also be imprinted in the mind of the breeder as he or she plans each mating, regardless of whether the progeny are to be shown or used for hunting. In fact, the Beagle standard was developed and approved by the National Beagle Club of America, whose mission since its inception in 1887 has been "to improve the Beagle in the field and on the bench." Therefore, the standard describes not only a beautiful hound, but one who has been designed to do his job both effectively and tirelessly.

The Official Standard For The Beagle

The following is the standard approved by the American Kennel Club in 1957.

Head—The skull should be fairly long, slightly domed at the occiput, with cranium broad and full. *Ears*—Ears

set on moderately low, long, reaching when drawn out
nearly, if not quite, to the end of the nose; fine in tex-
ture, fairly broad—with almost entire absence of erec-
tile power—setting close to the head, with the forward
edge slightly inturning to the cheek—rounded at the
tip. *Eyes*—Eyes large, set well apart—soft and hound-
like—expression gentle and pleading; of a brown or
hazel color. *Muzzle*—Muzzle of medium length—
straight and square-cut—the stop moderately defined.
Jaws—Jaws level. Lips free from
flews; nostrils large and open.
Defects—A very flat skull, narrow
across the top; excess of dome,
eyes small, sharp or terrier-like,
or prominent and protruding;
muzzle long, snipy or cut away
decidedly below the eyes, or
very short. Roman-nosed, or
upturned giving a dish-faced
expression. Ears short, set on
high or with a tendency to rise
above the point of origin.

*This hound is
waiting his
turn to go in
the ring at a
dog show.*

Body—Neck and Throat—Neck rising free and light
from the shoulders, strong in substance yet not loaded,
of medium length. The throat clean and free from
folds of skin; a slight wrinkle below the angle of the jaw,
however, may be allowable. *Defects*—A thick, short
cloddy neck carried on a line with the top of the shoulders. Throat showing dewlap and folds of skin to a
degree termed "throatiness."

Shoulders and Chest—Shoulders sloping—clean,
muscular, not heavy or loaded—conveying the idea of
freedom of action with activity and strength. Chest
deep and broad, but not broad enough to interfere
with the free play of the shoulders. *Defects*—Straight,
upright shoulders. Chest disproportionately wide or
with lack of depth.

Back, Loin and Ribs—Back short, muscular and
strong. Loin broad and slightly arched, and the ribs
well sprung, giving abundance of lung room. *Defects*—

Very long or swayed or roached back. Flat, narrow loin, flat ribs.

Forelegs and Feet—*Forelegs*—Straight with plenty of bone in proportion to the size of the hound. Pasterns short and straight. *Feet*—Close, round and firm. Pad full and hard. *Defects*—Out at elbows. Knees knuckled over forward, or bent backward. Forelegs crooked or Dachshund-like. Feet long, open or spreading.

Hips, Thighs, Hind Legs and Feet—Hips and thighs strong and well muscled, giving abundance of propelling power. Stifles strong and well let down. Hocks firm, symmetrical and moderately bent. Feet close and firm. *Defects*—Cowhocks, or straight hocks. Lack of muscle and propelling power. Open feet. *Tail*—Set moderately high; carried gaily, but not turned forward over the back; with slight curve; short as compared with size of the hound; with brush. *Defects*—A long tail. Teapot curve or inclined forward from the root. Rat tail with absence of brush.

Beagle breeders use the standard as a blueprint for what their dogs should look like.

Coat—A close, hard, hound coat of medium length. *Defects*—A short, thin coat, or of a soft quality.

Color—Any true hound color.

General Appearance—A miniature Foxhound, solid and big for his inches, with the wear-and-tear look of the hound that can last in the chase and follow his quarry to the death.

Varieties—There shall be two varieties:

Thirteen Inch—which shall be for hounds not exceeding 13 inches in height.

Fifteen Inch—which shall be for hounds over 13 but not exceeding 15 inches in height.

Disqualification—Any hound measuring more than 15 inches shall be disqualified.

You can see that the standard is fairly specific in some cases and rather open-ended in others, but that the authors had a clear idea of what a Beagle should be.

Various Types of Beagles

Today there are several distinct "types" of Beagles in this country, and considerable variety is available to the new Beagle owner in terms of size, appearance, temperament and inherited hunting ability, but a working understanding of the standard will give you some idea of what the breeder of your puppy considers most

The Beagle's eyes reveal honesty, loyalty, affection and intelligence.

important. For example, if he or she has no hounds in the establishment who look anything like the ideal, it is safe to conclude that showing is not a priority.

If the population in the kennel is significantly below the standard, it is questionable whether these hounds would be suitable for serious fieldwork. In extreme cases, they may even be unsuitable in the least demanding of pet homes, where serious conformational defects may lead to health problems.

Reviewing the Standard

If we examine the standard in more detail, we may find it interesting to note that color and markings are not considered important. There is a saying "A good horse cannot be a bad color," and this applies to Beagles as well. Beagles come in many colors, including the most common black, tan and white; lemon and white; red and white; chocolate (or liver), tan and white; and some colors whose names come from out of the hunting past, like "Belvoir (oddly enough, pronounced "beaver") Tan" and "Badger Pie."

Many of the Beagles appearing in photos taken in this country early in this century were predominately white, with the occasional patch of color, but the majority of today's Beagles are black, tan and white, with a tendency to have solid black backs, which is described as being "black blanketed." If a hound has flecks of color either tan (red) or muted black (blue), this coloring is called *ticking*, and when one refers to a "Blueticked" Beagle, the name refers only to the coloration and not to the Coonhound of the same name.

It is understandable why the authors of the standard would put such emphasis on the body and running gear of our little hounds. Originally they were expected to hunt for hours over all types of terrain, to overtake through courage, patience and persistence a hare capable of reaching speeds of forty miles per hour.

Not able to attain speeds like that themselves, the little hounds had to use their highly developed sense of smell, pack instincts and intelligence to stay in the chase till their quarry tired. Therefore all the emphasis is on strength, propelling power, sound, firm feet, freedom of action, ample lung capacity and other elements decidedly structural rather than cosmetic.

Why, then, so many points for the head? Well, when the cranium is described as "full and broad," we are of course assuming it is to be full of *brains*, and the wide nostrils and moderately long muzzle should help with the olfactory wizardry required of a hound expected to follow the

THE AMERICAN KENNEL CLUB

Familiarly referred to as "the AKC," the American Kennel Club is a nonprofit organization devoted to the advancement of purebred dogs. The AKC maintains a registry of recognized breeds and adopts and enforces rules for dog events including shows, obedience trials, field trials, hunting tests, lure coursing, herding, earthdog trials, agility and the Canine Good Citizen program. It is a club of clubs, established in 1884 and composed, today, of over 500 autonomous dog clubs throughout the United States. Each club is represented by a delegate; the delegates make up the legislative body of the AKC, voting on rules and electing directors. The American Kennel Club maintains the Stud Book, the record of every dog ever registered with the AKC, and publishes a variety of materials on purebred dogs, including a monthly magazine, books and numerous educational pamphlets. For more information, contact the AKC at the address listed in Chapter 13, "Resources," and look for the names of their publications in Chapter 12, "Recommended Reading."

trail of the rabbit, the game animal that leaves the least amount of scent of any quarry.

What about the concern about the *eyes*? Again, we may speculate that part of the reason derives from the Foxhound, of which our Beagle is a "miniature." Masters of Foxhounds were also horsemen, and the "kind eye" is one measure of a trustworthy mount. Regardless of the origin of this element of the stan-
dard, the "typical" Beagle expression is one of the things that makes the Beagle so compelling. If eyes are, indeed, the windows to the soul, then looking into a Beagle's eyes should reveal the honesty, loyalty, affection and intelligence that make the Beagle so beloved in the field, in the home and in the show ring. These eyes are also responsible for Beagles being given too many treats, but we will discuss that later.

The Beagle was built to hunt for hours over all types of terrain.

The key to evaluating a Beagle's conformation is in assessing the overall picture. Basically, a good Beagle will be "square" in appear-
ance; have good bone; a straight front; a deep chest with a pronounced "tuck-up"; strong, well-angulated hindquarters; and a good head with a pleasing expression. There should be symmetry and fluidity in his motion. Proportion and balance are important dimensions in assessing good Beagle type (it is possible to have a hound with acceptable parts that just are not knit together properly). Very often, a relative novice to the breed can select the best hound in a show ring or the best puppy in a litter just by assessing proportion and balance.

Disqualifying Faults

Perfection aside, let's talk about disqualifying faults.

One of the most common faults in today's field-bred Beagles used for brace trials is the tendency to become Basset-like.

Brace beaglers, wishing to slow their hounds down due to a current fad in that type of competition, have produced very heavy-boned, long-bodied hounds with none of the agility and grace of their ancestors. Because the length of time these hounds are under judgment on game is a matter of minutes, these conformational defects do not act as a liability as they would in a day's hunting, but these hounds are definitely more prone to back injuries.

William Bobbitt with some of his Glenbarr Beagles at the Bryn Mawr Hound Show. They are red and white, an uncommon but not unallowable color combination.

Along with the heavy bone (excessive) and long backs, crooked legs and open, or splayed, feet are common. Also, large heads and legs too short in relation to the body are common. Whereas field trials are a totally separate form of competition from dog shows, the new Beagle owner may still be confused by how distinctly different the types have become.

Other faults that occur may appear singly in an otherwise good-looking Beagle. There is another complex of faults that appears in some strains referred to as "weediness," which describes a hound with insufficient substance or bone, a weak head, short ears, terrier-like eyes and hare feet. This is to be avoided.

If you are wondering about your Beagle and where he fits into this continuum of structure and beauty, you can begin with the person who bred your puppy. Most responsible breeders are true Beagle fanatics and are happy to share what they have learned over the years with a new owner, both for your benefit and for the good of your puppy. Next, your veterinarian can usually let you know whether something is really wrong structurally. But basically, although there may be many types of Beagles, all have that inherent Beagle appeal and an inner beauty all their own.

The Beagle's Ancestry

A 1946 champion Beagle, Mulberry Farm Ben.

A common enough trait in the human population is the desire to search back in time to find ancestors—real or imagined—to give us a better sense of who we are, where we came from and, by extension, where we are going. In the process, we are apt to find poets and horse thieves, Indian princesses and corrupt politicians. If the history is long enough, it will be clouded enough by time for the historian to be selective and even creative about what is reported and how the events of the past are interpreted.

Unravelling the Beagle's Past

So it is with the history of the Beagle. Some people would like to claim that the Beagle was Adam's hunting dog (but not his food taster), and others would prefer that the Beagle, like Topsy, "just growed," leaving the historical antecedents of the modern Beagle to fend for themselves.

Somewhere in between these two camps, we should be able to recreate a satisfactory history of today's Beagle. Those who would prefer a more exhaustive history can repair to the library and find volumes to sift through. (See page 34 for more books and other information on the Beagle.) Those who care only about what is happening today will survive, I hope, this abridged version of Beagle History 101.

As stated previously, the Beagle is a scenthound bred over the centuries to hunt hare. We say *hare* rather than *rabbit* because in Europe and England, where much of this history took place, it is the European hare that is the quarry. It is fairly safe to state that the Beagle has evolved or been altered by centuries of selective breeding more than the hare has been, so perhaps a word about how the hare helped create the Beagle would be in order.

Weighing between eight and ten pounds, and possessed of great speed (up to forty miles per hour), the hare is a formidable game animal. It has a wide range and, with the exception of a few blips on the curve, has maintained a reasonable population level over the centuries.

Honing the Hunting Hound

In ancient times small dogs were used to hunt the hare, but, as the object was meat on the table rather than sport, not much consideration was placed on type or style of hunting. Basically the dogs helped locate the hare, a creature of open fields, and drove it into long nets for capture. There are written records of such hunts in Ancient Greece, predating the birth of Christ.

Even in the beginning, two distinct classes of canine were used to hunt the hare (or other quarry): scent-hounds, like the Beagle; and sight (or "gaze") hounds, like the modern Greyhound and Whippet. The former were members of sizeable packs, and the latter hunted either singly or in very small groups. Once the immediate necessity of meat on the table was solved, the "long dogs" (sight hounds) were used for a sport known as coursing, still very popular in the British Isles. In the U.S., the sport changed rather dramatically to Greyhound racing and moved to the track. But now sight hounds are again coursing for sport in open fields at AKC events.

The Beagle was subject to changes as well—many of them due to what could be called a "trickle-down effect" in the world of hounds.

From Deer to Hare

In England, the deer belonged to the King (remember Robin Hood?), and the most noble form of venery (hunting) was stag hunting. Large hounds similar to modern Foxhounds were the hound of choice. If you weren't King but were "landed" well enough to maintain hounds, horses and the staff to care for both, you had the option of hunting the ever-abundant and (much demonized) fox, which was considered vermin and therefore not worthy of royal attention. At the bottom of this ladder were the lesser noblemen who were still keen to hunt but may have lacked the resources or country to support a pack of Foxhounds. These became the first modern beaglers.

WHERE DID DOGS COME FROM?

It can be argued that dogs were right there at man's side from the beginning of time. As soon as human beings began to document their existence, the dog was among their drawings and inscriptions. Dogs were not just friends, they served a purpose: There were dogs to hunt birds, pull sleds, herd sheep, burrow after rats—even sit in laps! What your dog was originally bred to do influences the way it behaves. The American Kennel Club recognizes over 140 breeds, and there are hundreds more distinct breeds around the world. To make sense of the breeds, they are grouped according to their size or function. The AKC has seven groups:

1) Sporting, 2) Working,
3) Herding, 4) Hounds,
5) Terriers, 6) Toys,
7) Nonsporting

Can you name a breed from each group? Here's some help: (1) Golden Retriever; (2) Doberman Pinscher; (3) Collie; (4) Beagle; (5) Scottish Terrier; (6) Maltese; and (7) Dalmatian. All modern domestic dogs (*Canis familiaris*) are related, however different they look, and are all descended from *Canis lupus*, the gray wolf.

When we say the Beagle is a miniature Foxhound, implicit in that statement is that the history of the Beagle is inextricably intertwined with that of the evolution of the Foxhound, and the two matured about the same time—roughly 200 years ago.

Issues about standardizing the size, type and hunting style were thrashed about for years, and it is interesting to note that many of the same issues are hotly debated in the world of Beagles today: How fast should a hound be? What is the best size? Which is more important, nose or looks?

As an example, at one point when the hare population was on an extended down cycle, it was considered best to find a hare and hunt it as long as possible, since you may only find that one. Local country folk were paid for "hare spotting," and the hounds selected for this type of hunting were so meticulous and keen-nosed that it was said they could hunt a line in the morning, stop for lunch, and return two hours later to a marked line and continue hunting until dark!

Champion Robino III, painted by G. Muss Arnolt in 1905.

Finnicky or Fast?

By comparison, years later when hares were plentiful and farmers were complaining of crop damage, a hound was sought who could catch as many hares in a day as possible. This paralleled the breeding of Foxhounds, who also were being bred for more speed and drive and their ability to eliminate the foxes that were a liability to farmers raising livestock.

So, consistent with a present-day clash of ideals in what a working hound should be was the debate over which hound was superior for hunting the hare: the slow, toiling Southern Hound type (for the distinct breed of the Southern Hound had long since disappeared) or the so-called Northern Hound, possessed of greater speed and agility, but a different style of hunting entirely.

With a number of packs hunting in different parts of the country, with different terrain and agricultural practices, Beagle diversity is likely to have reached its peak before the advent of motor cars or even semiconvenient railway travel, when it became easier for packs to get together and compare notes.

The Beagle in America

In America, the Beagle kept a rather low profile until the mid-19th century. Actually, a popular favorite of the colonists was the Black-and-Tan Hound, a close relative of the modern Kerry Beagle of Ireland, more Foxhound or Harrier-sized, but a multipurpose hound capable of hunting small and large game, day or night.

The rabbit hound of that time was probably not much to look at, resembling a Dachshund more than a modern Beagle. But, then, consider the needs of the early settlers: A hound who helped put meat on the table was of primary importance, and in fact, the first naturalists to visit this country were perplexed by the common cottontail. It was neither a rabbit, living in warrens like the European rabbit (which was actually imported from Africa), nor was it a true hare, which lives its entire life aboveground, bears its young aboveground and is "precocious." The American cottontail lives aboveground most of the time, but takes refuge in holes, and also bears its young aboveground. But unlike the young hare (called a leveret), the young cottontail is born blind and helpless.

Meanwhile, the Foxhound is doing just fine, thank you, with advocates no less influential than George Washington, who continued foxhunting through much of the Revolutionary War!

Also, several distinct American strains of Foxhounds were being developed to match the different conditions seen on this continent.

The improvement of the American Beagle began in earnest with the importation in the mid- to late-19th century of foundation stock from the best working packs in England.

General Richard Rowett of Illinois was the first to begin this trend, and it was beaglers like Gen. Rowett, who were interested in a beautiful, functional hound, who formed the core group of breeders who were to develop the present standard (which is actually little different from the English standard) and form the club known today as the National Beagle Club of America.

As with any breed, there were those breeders who were able to maintain large numbers of animals and thereby have a greater opportunity to have an impact on the breed. So it is not surprising that in the records of the early winners both in the field and in the shows, the packs registered with the NBC did extremely well.

Competing with Beagles

The first Beagle field trial was held in Hyannis, Massachusetts, in 1888, one year after the formation of the NBC, and Beagle field trials have been going strong ever since. Beagle specialty shows began soon after, in 1891, and while there may have been less than a total meeting of the minds between the two groups, there were numerous individuals and packs that strove to "do it all."

Beagle lovers have always wanted beautiful, functional hounds.

Early into the 20th century, beaglers in New England who hunted the Varying Hare (Snowshoe Hare) developed their own form of testing hound merit by casting the entire class of hounds entered and competing them in a large pack for up to twelve hours. Whereas the cottontail is a creature given to short bursts, who will run in a reasonably small territory for a short interval before seeking sanctuary in a stone wall or groundhog den, its big-footed cousin will stay above-ground and run almost indefinitely, often taking the hounds out of the hearing range of their handlers for an hour or more.

This type of competition rewarded stamina, sound constitution and also sound temperament, to a certain extent, since many hounds cannot tolerate the pressure of a large pack of hounds in full cry. Of course the number of these trials was limited to the areas of the country where the Varying Hare was located.

A Beagle pack in full cry on the scent of a rabbit.

A subjective review of the period would suggest that the real hey-day of the Beagle in America was in the 1940s and '50s, when the sport of beagling and AKC registration of the Beagle grew exponentially. There was still sufficient open country that it was practical for many sportsmen to keep a few Beagles for hunting the ever-plentiful cottontail and the reasonably abundant pheasant. Beagle clubs were popping up all over the country, with field trials at the club level that enticed rabbit hunters to enter their "brag dogs" and thereby enter the world of organized beagling.

The show Beagle had reached an amazing degree of refinement, even relative to hounds bred a decade before, and still there were breeders able to produce hounds capable of earning their championship in both AKC field trials and bench shows—thereby earning the ultimate title of Dual Champion (DC). In addition to that, numerous hounds were completing their Field Championship with wins both in brace trials on the tricky cottontail, and large pack trials on the elusive and long-running Varying Hare.

Also at this time, the NBC held its trials for its recognized packs (sometimes known as formal packs, because of the traditional livery of green coats and white trousers worn by the hunt staff) during the same week it held its brace trial, often using the same judges for both events, and then a bench show for hounds who competed in the pack classes. The week of beagling would end with a three-hour Stake class, which tested a hound's endurance, nose and ability to cooperate as well as compete with other hounds. Some of the famous Beagle packs like the Vernon Somerset, the Sandanona, the Wolver and the Sir Sister competed in AKC field trials, bench shows (including the Pack classes at the Westminster Kennel Club,) and America's premier hound show, the Bryn Mawr Hound Show.

Splitting Field and Show Beagles

Aside from those few breeders dedicated to the dual-purpose hound, the gap grew ever wider between

The debate has long raged over hunting dogs: What is more important, nose or looks?

the field trial Beagle and the Beagle bred strictly with showing in mind. Sometime in the 1960s, a trend began in brace trials (the most popular form of competition at the time) to slow down the action.

The number of hounds competing in many of the most popular trials was so large that insufficient time was allocated to judge them as they would be judged under normal hunting conditions (that is, an entire day afield), so a more conservative hound who moved more slowly and thereby made fewer errors (remember the Southern Hound?) was favored over the faster, flashier hound who needed more time to settle down.

While there had been a number of famous field trial bloodlines then, such as Blue Cap, Yellow Creek, Shady Shore and Fish Creek, to name only a few, there were still hounds who earned their titles by *driving* a rabbit and outfooting their competition.

And Then Came Boogie

All that changed with the appearance of a hound named FC (Field Champion) Wilcliffe Boogie. Boogie captured the beagling public's imagination like few other hounds ever have, and while there is no question that he was a *hunting* hound (he was used to hunt raccoon, fox and rabbits), he was a trailing type hound. So while other famous hounds, like FC Gray's Linesman, were trailing hounds as opposed to driving hounds, people almost immediately began to linebreed and inbreed to Boogie, thereby fixing and even intensifying the driving trait.

Today the modern brace trial Beagle is a slow trailing specialist. In most cases a single heat of a competition may last only a few minutes and cover less than 100 feet. The dog is judged for the absence of any mistakes rather than actual accomplishment in pursuing the rabbit.

The modern large-pack-on-hare hound has changed little over the years. He still must have the stamina and constitution to compete, although the time on game has been reduced. Few new clubs have been formed for this type of trial, again because of the geographical limitations of the natural range of the Snowshoe Hare.

In the early 1970s, a group of beaglers unhappy with the trend in American Kennel Club brace trials began meeting with representatives of the AKC to persuade them to acknowledge a different form of competition that would more closely simulate hunting conditions. Hounds would be run in small packs, required to search for their own game and tested for gun-shyness. This type of trial, known as small pack option (SPO), is the fastest growing phase of the sport of beagling today. One of the larger SPO groups—the United Beagle Gundog Federation—conducts trials where the grand final winner is determined by combining his scores from both the field and the bench portion of the trial, a real step forward in improving the total Beagle.

America's Favorite Pet

The pet Beagle in America has, in many ways, been a by-product of both field-bred and show-bred beagles. No serious breeder breeds a bitch just for the sake of selling the puppies, and he or she usually has a clear objective in mind. Show-bred puppies who the breeder guesses won't make the grade, or field-bred puppies who turn out too large or small to fit the breeder's program, end up in pet homes. Assuming the breeder is

This is Corky, a top drug-sniffing dog with the U.S. Navy. Corky's sniffed out over 470 drug dealers in his career.

concerned with temperament, either type makes a suitable pet, but personally I'd be inclined to lean toward one with good looks, too.

In the not-too-distant past, it was common for "Dad's hunting dog" to be the family pet, to live in the house. This was also a time when more people lived on farms and Beagles lived a more liberated existence. Today, of course, a free-roaming Beagle would have a very short life expectancy, so many hunting Beagles live in outdoor kennels. I would like, however, to dispel the common myth among hunters that hunting Beagles are ruined by living in the house. If reasonable care is

taken in proper feeding, exercise and training, the Beagle better affiliated with his owner by virtue of more regular contact is more likely to perform better in the field than his counterpart in the backyard.

A Knowledgeable Nose

Aside from hunting, field trials and shows, Beagles have done well in recent years in Obedience Trials, and it seems that show and field lines perform equally well. Also, because of his small size, good disposition and outstanding sense of smell, the Beagle has been used by the United States Department of Agriculture at international airports to sniff out illegally imported foodstuffs or plants, which could introduce animal or plant diseases into this country. Beagles who do this work are part of the USDA's Beagle Brigade. The cheerful little Beagle goes about his job without frightening the travelers and can fit into some tight spots a larger animal could not squeeze into.

Another use of the Beagle in recent years has been in the detection of termites. Again, his small stature allows him to sniff around foundations and crawl spaces, and, unlike his human counterparts, he never begs for a raise!

The Beagle has proven to be extremely adaptable over the years, and that quality is undoubtedly one of the keys to his consistent popularity. This suggests that his future will be as interesting as his illustrious past.

chapter 3

The **World**
According to the
Beagle

If it can be said that a hawk's "world view" is shaped by its remarkable visual acuity, or that many prey animals' lives depend on their keen sense of hearing, then it can safely be said that the Beagle experiences much of the world through her nose. Once again we need only look to her origins to understand this develop-

ment. The noble Staghound, regal as he may be in the social hierarchy of hounds, frankly can't hold a candle to our little hounds in the nose department. Most dogs can follow the scent trail of a deer, and I know a number of humans who claim to be able to detect the presence of deer by the musky scent left behind in their "bunks." Similarly, the Foxhound has a more odoriferous quarry to contend with, and many humans with rather ordinary proboscises can detect the almost "skunky" spoor of the fox.

Not so, however, with the rabbit and hare, who give off the least amount of scent of any game animal. Therefore, although the Beagle has an extraordinarily well-developed sense of smell, she still has to work hard! This she does, and while the new owners of a Beagle puppy may find it amusing that the tiny creature cruises around the house with her nose to the ground, this is both a legacy from her pack-hunting ancestors and a rehearsal for future hunting if allowed the opportunity. Within days of settling into her new home, a Beagle will have memorized a rather detailed olfactory map of her territory, and her "rounds" each day will tell her whether anyone new has been round.

A Gregarious Fellow

Remember, the Beagle has been bred to live as a member of a *pack*. This has had several positive effects on the Beagle as a breed and subsequent benefits for today's Beagle owner.

The Beagle is gregarious; no kennelman caring for a large kennel of hounds would tolerate a fighter, so over the years, the aggressive characters have been eliminated as quickly as they appeared. Most hunting kennels had large lodging rooms with communal sleeping quarters and large exercise yards. There could be twenty or more hounds in each run, generally

---

A DOG'S SENSES

Sight: With their eyes located farther apart than ours, dogs can detect movement at a greater distance than we can, but they can't see as well up close. They can also see better in less light, but can't distinguish many colors.

Sound: Dogs can hear about four times better than we can, and they can hear high-pitched sounds especially well. Their ancestors, the wolves, howled to let other wolves know where they were; our dogs do the same, but they have a wider range of vocalizations, including barks, whimpers, moans and whines.

Smell: A dog's nose is his greatest sensory organ. His sense of smell is so great he can follow a trail that's weeks old, detect odors diluted to one-millionth the concentration we'd need to notice them, even sniff out a person under water!

Taste: Dogs have fewer taste buds than we do, so they're likelier to try anything—and usually do, which is why it's especially important for their owners to monitor their food intake. Dogs are omnivores, which means they eat meat as well as vegetable matter like grasses and weeds.

Touch: Dogs are social animals and love to be petted, groomed and played with.

separated by sex, so the importance of sound temperament cannot be underestimated.

While our modern Beagle may be a member of a pack consisting of himself and your family, his temperament is predictably excellent (assuming, of course, he is well treated), and his loyalty, courage and devotion have remained unchanged over the centuries.

Let me give you an example that demonstrates these qualities. Several years ago one of my favorite bitches was having a difficult labor, and the vet was called out to the kennel in the middle of the night. When he began doing a procedure that caused the expectant mother to cry out, we were startled to hear an ominous growl, then a ferocious warning bark, from behind us. "Lola," an otherwise gentle and quiet young hound, was letting us know in no uncertain terms that this was her kennelmate and we'd better not hurt her!

Bred to live and work in packs, the Beagle is cooperative, friendly and devoted. These are the Hills Bridge Beagles, Margaret Addis, Master of Beagles.

Another serendipitous by-product of this way of breeding and kennelling hounds over the centuries is that they have been bred to tolerate extended periods of downtime in between periods of exercise. In other words, Beagles today do not need extensive periods of exercise on a daily basis the way some of the more highly strung breeds may.

While it is true that many kennelmen "walked out" the pack once or even twice a day, many of their modern counterparts, faced with the realities of making a living in a much faster paced life, are lucky to be able to take hounds out once or twice a week. So, it is possible that a Beagle living in an apartment in the city may get as much exercise as his counterpart living in the countryside, especially if his owner likes to walk or jog.

27

Alive with the Sound of Music

The Beagle is possessed of a very musical voice (in fact the term used to describe the unique utterance of a particular hound in a pack is its "note"), and while not "yappy," the Beagle can be quite vocal in expressing himself, especially if a stray dog or cat enters his territory. This characteristic has led many people to praise the Beagle's usefulness as a watchdog; he will alert his owners when strangers are around, but he is not likely to kill the UPS man! Also, since he has been selectively bred for his voice as well as his nose, his alarm or warning bark often sounds like it has come from a much larger dog—a deterrent to would-be intruders.

The down-side to all this hound heritage is a tendency sometimes to be a bit headstrong, and cases of selective hearing in Beagles is not uncommon. If a Beagle is following a trail or just sniffing something really interesting, he will not be as likely to respond as if he were in the house—he is hearing "inner voices"! A knowledgeable Beagle owner will plan for these contingencies as part of his ongoing training.

Beagles are as content to lounge as they are to hunt.

Another "hound habit" is rolling in foul-smelling matter. While many breeds do this, it seems that Beagles, again because of their good noses, find more of it to roll in. Often they are just as inclined to eat such things, and if it weren't so disgusting, it would be funny, watching the litle reprobates trying to decide whether to eat or roll! Of course, in a kennel situation, such an event is no big deal, but for a house pet it usually means an unscheduled bath.

Experts think that the wild ancestors of the domestic dog engaged in this practice to mask their scent while hunting, and this in as likely a rationale as any, but when you closely examine the blissful look on their faces as they annoint themselves, you have to wonder whether something else might be going on!

Your Beagle's Attitude

There is a fairly wide range of temperament in today's Beagle, largely because there is such diversity among breeders and what each considers most important. Beagles bred for show, on average, tend to be bolder than their field-bred counterparts. On the face of it, this seems counter-intuitive, since one thinks of "hunting dogs" as bold, or even aggressive, but I have known many superb hunting Beagles who were quite shy. A shy show Beagle, on the other hand, would never stand a chance in the ring if he were constantly worried

about the presence of strangers, especially when one of them is the judge. Obviously, what we want is a bold, friendly little hound not too wary of strangers, but not too overbearing either.

Beagles enjoy activities like agility, obedience and tracking, but don't need that much exercise.

This story will take you into the inner workings of the Beagle.

Daisy, the Typical Beagle

Daisy half wakes up and yawns on the couch where she has been curled up most of the afternoon. She is very careful not to be caught napping on it when her

29

people are around, as she is apt to be scolded, but she has seen the ancient housecat do it for the past year with impunity, so she takes her chances. At almost three years old, she never causes any major problems around the house; her puppy teething ended when she was about a year old, she was well housebroken by six months old, she never has accidents (she can't say that for the cat!), and she no longer feels upset being left alone when her people are at work.

Some days they leave her outdoors in the fenced back-yard, where she has a house she can retreat into if it starts to rain, but now it is early spring, and the yard is wet and muddy. She is concerned that there may be something wrong with her people: they are always wiping her feet if she is muddy, and on those occasions when she is lucky enough to find something really mellow to roll in, they act like she has done something awful and give her a bath in something that smells so bad to her she can't wait to roll on the rug, the couch, or the fresh-cut lawn to get rid of it. And, of course, they still begrudge her those few tidbits she rescues from the trash.

> ## CHARACTERISTICS OF THE BEAGLE
>
> Experiences the world through his nose
>
> A family vs. a one-person dog
>
> Likes to use his voice
>
> Can be headstrong
>
> Likes to explore
>
> Doesn't need excessive exercise

She is getting progressively wakeful as the hour when her people generally return approaches. More cars are driving by, and suddenly one is approaching that she recognizes by its sound. She is waiting at the kitchen door as the car door slams, and the footsteps tell her it is her master. He comes in and doesn't notice her wagging her tail enthusiastically. His jacket is off and his necktie is askew and he is shuffling a stack of mail (many envelopes with picture windows!). He pulls the tie off the rest of the way and tosses it on the counter.

Getting His Attention

Not used to being ignored quite this much, she lightly rests her front paws on his leg and looks up expectantly.

She was discouraged from "jumping up" as a puppy, but somehow she is allowed to do this. Now she has his attention, as he bends down to stroke her under the chin, and follows up with an ear rub. "How was your day, Daisy? Busy protecting the homestead, or were you dreaming of rabbits all day?"

At the mention of the "R Word," her excitement level climbs, and instantly he realizes what he has done. Her vocabulary is not particularly large, but that word,

Beagles love to explore!

along with "biscuit," "treat" and her name all get predictable responses. He knows she would love to go for a run, and hasn't had much fun lately. Things have been busy on weekends, and until recently it has been pitch-dark when he returns from work.

Now, however, it appears there may be an hour or more of daylight remaining. He leaves his wife a note on the refrigerator, changes into jeans and an old sweater, and returns to the kitchen with her leash in hand. "So, do you want to chase a rabbit?" She begins squirming so from excitement that he has difficulty attaching the leash!

Time for Rabbits!

Only a couple of blocks away is the town's playground, a school and several playing fields. Abutting a couple of the fields is a small woodlot. It is early spring, approaching dusk, and, predictably, there is a cotton-tail rabbit nibbling the clover at the edge of the woods. Daisy does not see it, but her master, because of his height, does.

He lets her off the leash, and she bounds off towards the woods, her tail up and practically vibrating with

Welcome to
the World of
the Beagle

excitement. Soon she drifts over to where the cottontail was dining, and her whole body begins to wag! Her tail is whipping from side to side as she begins to whimper slightly, then breaks out into a Beagle aria!

Soon she is trotting along the line of scent left behind by the rabbit and singing her heart out with each track. Her master is grinning widely, watching his little rabbit specialist, and all the worries of the day are temporarily suspended.

A couple of kids interrupt their baseball game to investigate the commotion. "Hey, Mister, what's wrong with your dog?", asks one with great concern. This is not the first time he has been asked this, and even adults have confused the little hound's song of ecstasy with the sound of some creature in pain.

If your Beagle's on a scent, he may decide not to hear you calling!

"She is chasing a rabbit," he explains, and then answers the inevitable questions about whether she sees the rabbit (no), whether she will catch the rabbit (no, the rabbit will go into a hole if it gets too worried), whether she bites (no), and so on. All the while he is standing in one place and keeping track of the "hunt" by ear, only occasionally catching a glimpse of her in the woods. Suddenly, just as the kids are beginning to think he is making this all up, the rabbit pops out of the cover and almost runs into them before darting back into the woods. "Neat!" says one of the kids, "Excellent!" another.

Still Sniffing

A minute later, Daisy is in the open field, quiet now because the sudden change in terrain and change in direction have temporarily baffled her. Her nose is virtually vacuuming the short grass at the edge of the field when she finds the track and lifts her head in a long, musical note. The children are delighted, and if the truth were known, so is her master. The rabbit has completed one full circuit of its territory, and Daisy has successfully solved all its attempts to throw her off the trail. Before she can pursue it back into the woods, her master snaps her leash back on and praises her. The kids pet her, and she obviously likes the extra attention. It has turned out to be a good day for her.

Back home, her master checks her thoroughly for ticks, an almost year-round nemesis, then himself as well. Back in the kitchen as he prepares dinner, Daisy sits hopefully at his feet waiting for either a spill or a lapse in judgment. Her people have been warned by the spoilsport vet that she needs to watch her weight, especially now that she has been spayed. Her attentiveness has not been lost on him, and he asks whether she would like a treat.

Anything for a Treat

It sometimes amazes her that her people persist in asking such obvious questions, but she wags her tail, makes a halfhearted attempt at begging, and follows him to the cookie jar, where he extracts a small biscuit and tosses it to her. Her catch is flawless, as usual, and she retreats to her sanctuary under the kitchen table to savor this prize. Unknown to her, her master makes a mental note to adjust her next feeding to allow for this in-between-meal snack! He also makes a note to get her out running more often; it would keep both of them in better shape, especially if he ran along behind her, and besides, it is a perfect antidote for the stress of everyday modern life.

While the story of Daisy is a composite (and names have been changed to protect the innocent), it illustrates several things about the "soul" of a Beagle: They *love* to hunt, they are bonded to their packmates, (be they human or canine), they have a simple *joie de vivre*

that all of us could well emulate, and they love to eat.
In the latter instance, it has been said of Beagles that
death precedes anorexia, and while this may be some
small exaggeration, it is very close to the truth!

In short, the Beagle has a rather simple world view. He
is a hedonist (in the best sense of the word), a sports-
man, and a great proponent of "family values." What
more could one want in a Best Friend?

More Information on Beagles

NATIONAL BREED CLUB

National Beagle Club
Susan Mills Stone,
Corresponding Secretary
P.O. Box 13
Middleburg, VA 20118-0013
Web: http://clubs.akc.org/NBC/index.htm

The club can send you information on all aspects of
the breed, including the names and addresses of clubs
in your area. Inquire about membership.

BOOKS

Arne, Barbara. *Beagles*. Kansas City, Missouri: Andrews
McMeel Publishing, 1996.

Bennett, Bill. Training Basics: *Training of the Hunting
Beagle*. Sun City, Arizona: Doral Publishing, 1995.

Hansen, Geoff. *My Life as a Dog: The Many Moods of
Lucy, the Dog of a Thousand Faces*. Kansas City, Missouri:
Andrews McMeel Publishing, 1999.

Kraeuter, Kristine. *Training Your Beagle*. Hauppauge,
New York: Barrons Educational Series, 2001.

Singer, Marilyn and Clement Oubrerie. *It's Hard to
Read a Map with a Beagle on Your Lap*. New York: Henry
Holt & Co., 1997.

Vriends-Parent, Lucia. *Beagles: Everything About Purchase,
Care, Nutrition, Behavior and Training*. Hauppauge, New
York: Barrons Educational Series, 1995.

MAGAZINES

Better Beagling, Magazine of the Hunting Beagle
P.O. Box 8142
Essex, VT 05451
Phone (802) 878-3616
Fax: (802) 878- 0634
Web: www.betrbeagle.com/subscribe.htm
E-mail: info@betrbeagle.com

Small Pack Option Magazine
P.O. Box 569
Greene, NY 13778
(607) 656-5367

VIDEOS

Beagle Video
For Beagle enthusiasts who want to learn more about
the breed, check out this in-depth video featuring
breeders, trainers, and a veterinarian $24.95 from
Mind's Eye Productions
50 Ela Street
Barrington, IL 60004
(800) 570-3647
E-mail: mepvideo@aol.com
Web: www.petvideo.com/dachs.html

Shiloh
This 1997 film features a mistreated Beagle and the
quick-thinking boy next door who sets out to rescue
him. Starring Michael Moriarity. The 1999 sequel is
named *Shiloh 2: Shiloh Season.*

He's Your Dog, Charlie Brown/It's Flashbeagle
These classic animated works feature two Snoopy car-
toons. The first, *He's Your Dog, Charlie Brown*, was made
in 1968. The second of the two, *It's Flashbeagle*, is an
'80's era, disco dog take on the movie *Flashdance.*

Living

with a

part two

Beagle

chapter 4

Bringing Your
Beagle
Home

It would be useful, if only as a preparatory exercise, to consider the acquisition of your new Beagle as a marriage rather than a simple purchase. For one thing, as with humans, we have already seen how the family is as important as the individual. You will have a pretty good idea of what your puppy's potential will be once you have visited the kennel of origin and discussed the breeder's "world view" as it applies to Beagles and beagling.

Consider that visit the phase in a courtship where one goes with some trepidation to meet the future in-laws. Pay close attention to what the breeder has to say about his or her Beagles, the breeding program, and what he or she considers most useful or important in a Beagle.

38

Be Choosy Before You Buy

Pay close attention to the hounds in the kennel; whether they fit the breeder's word description of what Beagles are all about and, more importantly, whether they look and act like what you think you would like! There is considerable variety in Beagles in America today. Since your marriage with this hound may last longer than the average marriage among humans in modern times, it makes sense to go into it with both eyes open! It is not uncommon for a well-cared-for Beagle to live into her mid-teens, so selecting the right mate becomes very important.

The acquisition of a Beagle (or any puppy) represents a life change for many people. For a single person or a couple without children, it means there is now someone waiting at home who is totally dependent on you for her support and well-being. Young puppies, especially, have schedules that must be respected if they are to be housebroken, healthy and reasonably well-adjusted. Obviously, the important schedules of the breadwinners in the family must be taken into consideration, but, once established, these schedules should not be juggled about much—although a degree of flexibility is necessary.

We all know of people who insist on eating at the same times every day, retiring at the same hour, and so on, and while we may think of ourselves as more freewheeling types, we cannot impose our lifestyles on others without making them unhappy. Think of your puppy as your aged Uncle Fred who gets cranky if he doesn't eat dinner by a certain hour. It might be a minor inconvenience, but things will be much better for everyone if that timeline is met!

Raising a Baby Beagle

For people who have been responsible for the primary care of infants, this is all self-explanatory, and it is not uncommon for young couples to introduce a puppy into their relationship before bringing a human baby into it. I prefer not to think that our Beagles are used

PUPPY ESSENTIALS

Your new puppy will need:

food bowl

water bowl

collar

leash

I.D. tag

bed

crate

toys

grooming supplies

Living with a
Beagle

as tests to see whether one's mate can perform as a responsible caregiver, but as long as the puppy turns out alright and her human successor benefits, I suppose worse things have happened.

The acquisition of a Beagle puppy represents a life change.

The reason for the marriage and parenting analogies is based on my growing concern that Beagle owners not be a part of the growing problem of "quickie divorces" among dog owners who may treat puppies as disposable if they do not meet their unrealistic expectations, or no longer are convenient. Take the time to understand what dog ownership entails over the long haul, and understand, by reading this book and in any other way you can, what is unique about having a Beagle as a family member.

Having said all that, I should quickly say that Beagles are pretty easy to get along with. They are remarkably simple to care for, have even dispositions, eat little compared to the larger breeds, never complain about the cooking, and will be, over time, amazingly in tune with their owner's moods and energy levels. But that doesn't mean we should take them for granted or expect total flexibility from them, so let us look at what we have to do to become Beagle-ready.

Remember, all Beagle puppies are cute. Select a puppy, and ask the breeder to hold her for you until you are prepared. Most breeders will accept a deposit and keep a puppy for a few days if it will help create a marriage that will endure. A surprising number of Beagle breeders may not be totally familiar with counselling new owners on what is involved in surviving puppyhood—housetraining, obedience training, and becoming good canine citizens—because of their limited focus on what a Beagle can do, so it is important that you learn as much as you can about these things on your own.

Welcoming Your Puppy Home

Before the puppy comes home, examine your household as if you were "babyproofing." Even though you will not likely give your puppy free rein of the house, it is best to guard your valuables against the teething puppy, and remove anything from her reach that may be injurious or toxic. Anything small enough to be swallowed or that can be chewed or shredded until small enough to be swallowed needs to be removed.

Make sure you have a collar and leash for your Beagle.

Similarly, many common houseplants are toxic to dogs and cats, so keep them out of reach. Sprays can be applied to furniture items that will make them taste bad and therefore discourage chewing, but if you have something you especially value, keep it well hidden. Also, remember that electrical cords, when chewed, can prove fatal.

Using a Crate

Most trainers today advocate the use of the crate as a way of housetraining a new puppy. An added advantage is that the crate can later be used for travel or for those occasions when you wish the puppy to be in protective custody, like when little children are visiting. The principle, as it applies to housetraining, is that puppies are reluctant to eliminate where they sleep.

By the time your puppy is weaned, she will probably be eating three times a day. It is common for young puppies to eliminate after every meal, as well as after waking. Knowing this makes it possible, with some

planning and keen observation, to anticipate your
puppy's need to use the outdoors or newspaper,
depending on which venue you choose.

The crate must be only as large as you absolutely need
it to be, based on the anticipated size of your Beagle
at maturity. If the crate is too large, the puppy will
convert it into a two-room suite, making one part the
bedroom and the other part the bathroom.

*Your Beagle is a
unique member
of your family,
with her own
special needs.*

Don't feel bad about keeping your puppy in the crate
for reasonable periods of time. Most people do not
realize that young puppies, like babies, sleep a good
deal of the time. After relatively brief periods of training or play, your puppy will soon look forward to the
security her crate affords.

Collars, Leashes and Other Supplies

You will want to have a collar and leash ready before
you pick up your puppy, but don't expect to use them
much right away. The more gradually things happen,
the less stressful on both of you. Consequently, it is best
to get the puppy acclimated to the collar (a lightweight
nylon type is best for this stage) before using the leash.

The first encounter with the leash can be traumatic
sometimes, and some trainers, rather than letting the

puppy associate that unpleasantness with them, tie them up to a tie-out stake or some similar device and let them play themselves out and get used to the feel of both collar and leash before attempting to walk them. Lightweight and inexpensive are the keys here, as your Beagle will soon outgrow these puppy trappings.

Bowls, Beds and Toys

Similarly, when you consider such possessions as feeding bowls, beds and toys, keep in mind that what is appropriate for a mature Beagle may not be for a young puppy. A puppy's food and water bowls are better if they are more shallow than ones used for older animals, and while the puppy's bed is often an old rug or towel, you might prefer (once the accidents cease) something filled with an aromatic stuffing like cedar shavings, which will not only help keep her sweet-smelling but are reputed to help control fleas.

Your puppy will need to chew for much longer than you would like; chew toys are an acceptable alternative to your antiques. Ask your vet about what is both satisfying and safe for your pup. Toys made of rawhide or other organic matter are degradable and therefore can be ingested. Basically, all you want your puppy to swallow is her food, so be careful not to accidentally harm your puppy with these treats. As your puppy gets bigger and her digestive system matures, these things may come off the forbidden list, but, again, check with your vet.

HOUSEHOLD DANGERS

Curious puppies and inquisitive dogs get into trouble not because they are bad, but simply because they want to investigate the world around them. It's our job to protect our dogs from harmful substances, like the following:

IN THE HOUSE

cleaners, especially pine oil

perfumes, colognes, aftershaves

medications, vitamins

office and craft supplies

electric cords

chicken or turkey bones

chocolate

some house and garden plants, like ivy, oleander and poinsettia

IN THE GARAGE

antifreeze

garden supplies, like snail and slug bait, pesticides, fertilizers, mouse and rat poisons

---

43

Outdoor Time

As discussed before, the Beagle does not require a great deal of exercise, and this is especially true of little puppies. However, if you would like to institute a regimen involving walks, or, later, the occasional rabbit chase, try to be as consistent and regular as possible. If

you are lucky enough to have a fenced yard, a bench or doghouse with a flat roof will give your older puppy a chance to jump up, and in the process change her perspective on things. It will also give her a dry spot in which to sun herself when the ground may be damp or too cool to make her nap as restful as it could be.

Crates are great housetraining aids, as well as safe havens for a dog.

Once your puppy is close to her mature size (approximately six to eight months of age), you will want to replace the puppy collar, lead, and feeding bowls with something more age-appropriate. I personally prefer the traditional leather to the newer nylon items, but either type works well.

Don't Forget I.D.

Some supply houses offer free nameplates on both collars and leads, but even if that is an extra cost, I highly recommend them. The mandatory dog license from your municipality is not sufficient to guarantee your pet's safe return in the event she strays from home, but a nameplate secured to the collar with your name, address and phone number will help. Many people add "collect" or "reward" to the tag to encourage people to do the right thing.

The adult feeding bowls should be large enough for a full day's feed and water; beyond that, you are on your own as far as style and material. Try to think somewhat practically, however, and remember that your Beagle

can't read or see colors. Spill-proof is always a good option, especially for the water bowl, but dishwasher-proof is more important. Whereas it was always prescribed that bowls be regularly disinfected, today's high-temperature dishwashers make it feasible to wash your Beagle's dishes along with everyone else's.

Only after you have secured these things for your puppy, as well as the kind of food recommended by the breeder, are you ready to bring your new puppy home. It is best to do this at the beginning of a weekend or vacation, if possible, when you can spend some time bonding and getting to know each other. And, incidentally, don't expect a lot of sleep the first night or two.

Make sure your Beagle has appropriate chew toys at home.

chapter 5

Feeding
Your
Beagle

People today are extremely conscious about what they eat, or at least what they are supposed to eat, and studies are being published almost every week touting the magical properties of one foodstuff or another. Then along comes another study that would seem to contradict the findings of all the previous studies. In short, this business about nutrition is confusing, and, not surprisingly, many people throw up their hands and surrender to the oldest dietary demon of all—deceptive advertising!

Learn What You're Looking At

A similar situation exists with dog food, at least in the area of advertising, and the number of brands of commercial dog food, as well as all the different forms and formulations within each brand name, can be quite mind boggling. Ironically, it is likely that more is known about canine nutrition than about human nutrition, and the nutritional labels that have only recently found their way on human food products have been prominently displayed on dog food bags for many years.

Before delving too deeply into our modern dog food, however, let us take a look at how Beagles have been fed in the past. While dogs kept in or around homes were likely to have been fed tablescraps and therefore prospered or declined along with their human hosts, the business of feeding a pack of hounds was a more serious under-taking.

How Hounds Were Fed

In the larger hunting kennels, there was a separate job strictly devoted to preparing the feed for the hounds. It was a common belief that hounds, like their ancestor, the wolf, needed meat in large quanti-ties to maintain their fitness. Not much consideration was given to the later stages of life, because a hound's longevity was determined by his useful life in the pack.

HOW MANY MEALS A DAY?

Individual dogs vary in how much they should eat to maintain a desired body weight—not too fat, but not too thin. Puppies need several meals a day, while older dogs may need only one. Determine how much food keeps your adult dog looking and feeling her best. Then decide how many meals you want to feed with that amount. Like us, most dogs love to eat, and offering two meals a day is more enjoyable for them. If you're worried about overfeeding, make sure you measure correctly and abstain from adding tidbits to the meals.

Whether you feed one or two meals, only leave your dog's food out for the amount of time it takes her to eat it—10 minutes, for example. Freefeeding (when food is available any time) and leisurely meals encourage picky eating. Don't worry if your dog doesn't finish all her dinner in the allotted time. She'll learn she should.

Also, most packs were able to farm out their puppies with local supporters of the hunt (usually farmers), a practice known as sending the puppy out "at walk." This meant that in addition to the puppies being socialized by the farmer's family, exposed to livestock they would be taught not to chase, and protected from diseases as much as possible, they had access to "puppy food," like milk and cooked table scraps.

47

By the time a puppy returned to the kennel at about one year of age, he was ready for grown-up food. In most cases that consisted of meat mixed with a porridge of small grains. The kennelman would travel to the farms in the hunt's country and pick up sick, aged or dead livestock, bring it back to the kennel and prepare it for the hounds. The amount of meat in proportion to the gruel would be adjusted based on the amount of work the hounds were getting.

In summer, when hounds were not hunting, they would be getting a much less nutrient-dense feed, with the exception of the brood bitches. When hounds were hunting, and therefore getting more animal protein, they actually were allowed to adopt a more wolflike eating pattern of gorge-and-rest, usually being fed only three times a week.

Some Beagle kennels in England still feed "flesh," but in this country commercial dry dog food has obviated the need for a full-time feeder. Most Beagle hunting packs are still fed in large groups from troughs, so in order to prevent hounds from inhaling the dry food, it is soaked for a period of time and allowed to soften and expand. In all other types of Beagle kennels, hounds are likely to be fed individually from bowls, but a number of field trial kennels over the years have used self-feeders that allow the hounds to consume dry feed free-choice. Proponents of this latter system feel that most hounds will self-regulate

HOW TO READ THE DOG FOOD LABEL

With so many choices on the market, how can you be sure you are feeding the right food for your dog? The information is all there on the label—if you know what you're looking for.

Look for the nutritional claim right up top. Is the food "100% nutritionally complete"? If so, it's for nearly all life stages; "growth and maintenance," on the other hand, is for early development; puppy foods are marked as such, as are foods for senior dogs.

Ingredients are listed in descending order by weight. The first three or four ingredients will tell you the bulk of what the food contains. Look for the highest-quality ingredients, like meats and grains, to be among them.

The Guaranteed Analysis tells you what levels of protein, fat, fiber and moisture are in the food, in that order. While these numbers are meaningful, they won't tell you much about the quality of the food. Nutritional value is in the dry matter, not the moisture content.

In many ways, seeing is believing. If your dog has bright eyes, a shiny coat, a good appetite and a good energy level, chances are his diet's fine. Your dog's breeder and your veterinarian are good sources of advice if you're still confused.

and not overeat once they have been on the system for a while.

What's Best for Your Beagle

What complicates feeding our house Beagles so much is that we humans equate food with love, and our little hounds are too smart to tell us anything different. Consequently, we find ourselves letting our little pals lick our plates, eat the few odds and ends in the fridge we are suspicious or tired of, clean up the spills on the kitchen floor, and so on, until our once svelte little hound starts looking like an over-stuffed sausage! If we really love them, we will select a good quality, nutrient-dense dry dog food and feed nothing but that every day for the rest of their lives.

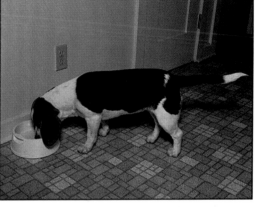

Beagles are hearty eaters; don't let yours con you into giving her extra tidbits!

As mentioned earlier, the Beagle has a wonderful appetite, and it is a rare Beagle who is a picky eater, compared to other small dogs. When people worry that their pet's diet is too boring, they are projecting their own feelings into a situation that is perfectly fine with the Beagle. The research kennels owned by the manufacturers of dry dog food house generations of animals who have lived and reproduced on nothing but dry food, often containing not much more than the minimum nutrient requirements as set forth by the American Association of Feed Control Officials (AAFCO). Also, even before the manufacture of dry dog food was as refined as it is today, thousands of field Beagles were fed diets as primitive as corn bread, "cracklin's" (the by-product of rendering lard), and the occasional meat scrap.

All this suggests that the Beagle has been pretty forgiving in his feeding requirements over the years. Our concern should be finding a food that is convenient to feed, is completely balanced so that no supplements are necessary, is nutrient-dense so that less food is consumed and therefore less stool volume is generated, and is reasonably priced so that we don't have to restructure our family grocery budget.

TYPES OF FOODS/TREATS

There are three types of commercially available dog food—dry, canned and semimoist—and a huge assortment of treats (lucky dogs!) to feed your dog. Which should you choose?

Dry and canned foods contain similar ingredients. The primary difference between them is their moisture content. The moisture is not just water. It's blood and broth, too, the very things that dogs adore. So while canned food is more palatable, dry food is more economical, convenient and effective in controlling tartar buildup. Most owners feed a 25% canned/75% dry diet to give their dogs the benefit of both. Just be sure your dog is getting the nutrition he needs (you and your veterinarian can determine this).

Semimoist foods have the flavor dogs love and the convenience owners want. However, they tend to contain excessive amounts of artificial colors and preservatives.

Dog treats come in every size, shape and flavor imaginable, from organic cookies shaped like postmen to beefy chew sticks. Dogs seem to love them all, so enjoy the variety. Just be sure not to overindulge your dog. Factor treats into her regular meal sizes.

Different Dogs Need Different Diets

There has been considerable research over the past few years to suggest that nutrient requirements change according to age, condition, activity level, gestation, lactation, and so on, and this only makes sense on an intuitive level. A hound who runs hundreds of miles a week hunting is going to burn more calories than a Beagle couch potato. Also, if that same hunting Beagle is kept in an unheated kennel, a certain number of calories will be used just to maintain body temperature.

While the protein requirements may not change that much, the energy difference must come either from additional carbohydrates or from fat. Fat has more calories on a dry-weight basis than either protein or carbohydrates, so it is the logical choice for supplementing the diets of hardworking animals. The Eskimos have known this for centuries, and their sled dogs (often pure Arctic wolves) consumed diets that were up to 60 percent fat! Today's sled dogs have the benefit of research in helping them compete in events like the Iditarod, where not only survival, but speed, endurance and ease of feeding are considerations.

Advances in feed manufacturing techniques have made it possible to incorporate higher levels of fat into extruded dog foods than in the past, thereby eliminating the need for the dog owner to add it on after the fact, which used to throw the correct nutritional proportions out of balance.

Do Dogs Need Meat?

There is considerable controversy as to whether dogs need meat at all, if all the necessary proteins and amino acids can be supplied by vegetable sources, such as soybean meal. Other people, feeling that dogs are carnivores, believe that meat is the single most important ingredient in their diets. There is probably a middle ground somewhere which recognizes that dogs are, in fact, omnivores and eat a variety of foodstuffs in the wild. In fact, wolves and wild dogs, when consuming prey animals, eat the entire thing, including the stomach contents (vegetation), fur (dietary fiber), bones (calcium and phosphorous), as well as the muscles and organs usually lumped under the general heading of "meat."

Types of Dog Food

There are a number of forms in which dog food is sold, the most common being dry, semimoist and canned. Dry dog food, as the name implies, contains little moisture and is crunchy. Semimoist products contain more moisture and are generally manufactured to simulate meat, which means that various gums and food coloring agents are used. Canned dog food may be mostly meat and meat by-products, or it may be a combination of vegetable and meat products. In any case, it is likely to contain up to 70 percent moisture.

Generally speaking, the canned foods are the most palatable, but they are also the most expensive on a dry-weight basis. Also, as people become more conscious of recycling, the presence of smelly cans becomes less attractive. I keep canned food on hand—it has a long shelf life—and use it on those rare occasions when an appetite stimulant is needed, as when a hound is recuperating from an illness or when I need to mask the taste of a medicine.

Some people have reported to me that the semimoist foods are handy when travelling, but frankly, what could be more convenient than taking along some of the pet's regular food? This would also reduce the stress associated with travel, changes in food and water, and so forth. Add to that the artificial coloring, and I'm hard pressed to make a case for this form of dog food.

TO SUPPLEMENT OR NOT TO SUPPLEMENT?

If you're feeding your dog a diet that's correct for her developmental stage and she's alert, healthy-looking and neither over- nor underweight, you don't need to add supplements. These include table scraps as well as vitamins and minerals. In fact, a growing puppy is in danger of developing musculoskeletal disorders by oversupplementation. If you have any concerns about the nutritional quality of the food you're feeding, discuss them with your veterinarian.

The Qualities of Kibble

This leaves dry dog food. Today you can find foods with high-quality meat-based protein sources like beef, lamb or chicken, or the less expensive soybean meal, corn glutton meal or various "by-products." You can find carbohydrate sources like wheat flour, corn meal or rice. The protein levels may be as low as 18 percent or as high as 30 percent. The fat levels may be as low as 5 percent or as high as 20 percent. How do you choose? One of the ways not to choose is based on the price on the bag.

There is general agreement that the closer the feed is to the "minimums," the lower the margin of error in guaranteeing that there will not be any deficiencies. On the other extreme, there are those who wonder what the long-term effects will be of "overnutrition" (feeding excess levels of protein), particularly on the kidneys.

Take the time to read the labels carefully. A $5 bag of food that requires you to feed two cups a day costs the same as a $10 bag of food that requires you to feed only one cup a day, and you will have less stool to contend with. While you can find a perfectly acceptable food at the supermarket, it is at the pet shops and feed stores that you are more likely to find premium brands—as well as people prepared to answer your questions about the brands they sell. Be sure to have them show you how to locate the encoded manufacture and expiration dates, which are printed on each bag. Vitamins degrade over time, and feeds may become stale, rancid, moldy (even if the spores are not visible to the naked eye), or "buggy," so freshness is important. For these same reasons, it is best not to buy too much feed at one time.

How Much to Feed?

If you take the recommendation of the breeder in selecting the food, keep in mind that the amounts they feed are based on the activity levels of their dogs in their geographical area. Similarly, the recommended feeding quantities as they appear on the bag are guidelines. Some Beagles will get fat on one cup of premium food a day, and another might require twice that just to keep his ribs from showing. This means you will have

You'll know your Beagle's getting what he needs in his diet if his skin and coat look good, his eyes are shiny, and he's full of energy, like these Bare Cove Beagles.

to use your own judgment after getting input from the vet, breeder and feed store.

A well-fed Beagle will always be a *bit* hungry, so that is not a clue as to the proper amount to feed. The rule of thumb as to whether your Beagle is the correct weight is that you

should be able to feel his ribs but not see them. If he is free of parasites and kept reasonably clean, there should be a "bloom" on his coat that comes with just the right amount of subcutaneous fat.

Should you feed the meal wet or dry? There are pluses and minuses to each method, and you will have to determine what works best for you and your Beagle. Feeding wet usually means either moistening or soaking the dry food in warm water or broth for a few minutes. I recommend this method for young puppies, whose dentition may not be up to crunching down their meals easily. Advocates of wet feeding believe it results in less bloating. It may also increase palatability and digestibility—considerations more important for puppies than for adults.

Dry feeding requires no time delay and may help slow down a hound who would otherwise gulp down his food. It may also be better for your pet's dental health. Also, on those rare occasions when your pet doesn't immediately clean his plate, you needn't be concerned with spoilage.

Keep Your Beagle Slim

Finally, remember that obesity will shorten your Beagle's lifespan, increase the likelihood of health problems, and in general reduce his quality of life. The occasional biscuit, bit of meat or cooked egg can be given as a special treat, but on the whole "tough love" will result in a happier, healthier Beagle.

chapter 6

Grooming
Your
Beagle

One of the things pet own-ers like best about Beagles is the fact that very little grooming is required to keep them looking clean and healthy. Whereas long-haired breeds require almost daily combing and brushing to keep untangled, and wire-coated breeds need to be clipped or plucked three or four times a year, our little hounds are

the quintessential low-maintenance canines.

Many hunting Beagles go an entire lifetime without seeing the inside of a grooming salon—or even the basement sink! Assuming they are properly fed and kept in a clean environment, the occasional "herbal bath" obtained by running them through wet vegetation keeps them shiny looking and sweet-smelling. Also, beaglers who use cedar shavings in the hound's sleeping quarters never have to worry about their Beagle offending anyone with "doggy" odor.

In the hunting kennels of old, a smelly, oily "dressing" was used to control external parasites and skin disease, but today sponge-on rinses or dips accomplish the same objective without the mess. We will discuss those in more detail in Chapter 7, but for now suffice it to say that grooming your Beagle, including that part of grooming which is designed to promote good health as well as good looks, need not require heroic measures.

Beagles are low maintenance dogs when it comes to grooming.

Keeping Clean Is Being Clean

The first essential in having a well-groomed Beagle is keeping her environment clean. When well-

intentioned but misinformed people tell you that Beagles are "smelly," it is usually because they have encountered members of the breed who were kept in less than optimal conditions.

It is a shame that some Beagle owners over the years have exiled their hounds to the backyard chained to a doghouse, where the bedding may have been changed infrequently and the area around the doghouse muddy or contaminated with feces.

Often this was done with the mistaken notion in mind that if the hound were allowed in the house she would be "ruined for hunting." The result usually is a Beagle who gets insufficient human interaction, and this is compounded when the kids stop playing with her because she is smelly.

Beagles who for whatever reason must spend any time out of doors should have a small weatherproof house with a removable roof to make it easy to clean, disinfect and change the bedding. Cedar shavings are purported to help reduce the flea population on your pet (in addition to being a pleasant canine cologne), but the less expensive pine shavings may be mixed in to economize.

Bathe Only for Beauty

It is not only unnecessary to bathe your Beagle, it is counterproductive, since it will rob the hound's skin of the oils and exacerbate the tendency of some house Beagles to have dry skin and the itchiness that goes with it. This is especially true in the winter, when the dry heated air in the house is a problem for humans as well.

Bathing should be reserved for emergencies only, such as when your friend has been sprayed by a skunk or has rolled in something malodorous. Even in the latter instance, time, drying and vigorous brushing may suffice. In the case of the skunk attack, the thorough soaking with tomato juice need not include soap or detergent and therefore more closely approximates "marinating" than bathing.

If your Beagle rolls in something stinky, you'll need to give her a bath.

When you do bathe your Beagle, use tepid water rather than hot, as dogs don't tolerate very warm water as well as we do. Use a commercial dog shampoo rather than something you have in your bathroom, and follow the directions on the bottle. While you are at it, you will probably want to use a shampoo that is effective against fleas and ticks, and most will have some kind of conditioner to put back some of the moisture inevitably removed by bathing.

Be sure to rinse thoroughly and keep your pet indoors
(except during the warm months) until thoroughly
dry. Even if the weather is warm enough to let your
Beagle "sun-dry," it is often better to confine her until
completely dry, as she is likely to go out of her way to
get dirty by rolling and rubbing up against everything
in sight for the first hour or so after a bath.

Be careful in bathing to avoid getting the suds or water
in your pet's eyes or ears. Some people put cotton or
mineral oil in the hound's ears and mineral oil or eye
ointment in the eyes before bathing, but I prefer to just
be careful.

*To keep your
Beagle looking
good, just brush
him regularly.*

When you are not bathing your Beagle—which should
be most of the time—regular grooming will consist of
frequent brushing. This routine is best established
while your puppy is small and if introduced properly
should be pleasurable for both you and your pet.

Brushing Works Wonders

Unlike the longhaired breeds whose coats are prone
to tangling and matting, the Beagle's coat must be
brushed more to bring out the shine and gently
stimulate the skin. For this purpose, a wire carding
brush is often used. With short wire bristles set in soft
rubber, this brush is gentle on the skin and is useful in

58

thinning the undercoat during those times when your hound is shedding.

Shedding blades, which resemble a looped saw blade with a handle, are also handy in removing dead hair during shedding. Some people have a personal preference for natural bristle brushes, and while these may not be as efficient as the other two tools described, efficiency is not the only consideration in grooming. It is also a time to bond with your pet, and therefore should feel good as well as make her look good. Many people report that quietly brushing their pet while relaxing on the couch or favorite armchair is very relaxing for them as well.

The Great Hound Glove

A fourth tool for regular grooming is the hound glove, a squarish-shaped mitten with short bristles on one side. Petting or massaging your Beagle with the hound glove on your hand meets her needs for human interaction and stroking, cleans her coat, and stimulates her skin at the same time. Current research suggests that people who have pets have fewer stress-related illnesses due, it is surmised, to the tranquilizing effects of stroking the pet, so these grooming sessions could be good for *both* of you!

Towels are commonly used in the grooming of hounds and, in addition to their obvious utility in tidying up the dog after a walk in the rain or snow, are often used as the final polishing tool after the brush and glove. The towel can also be lightly moistened with various pleasant-smelling insect repellents when called for and used to rub these medications into the coat in a way that is less upsetting to the hound than spray application would be.

A flea comb, a fine-toothed metal comb, is useful when fleas are a problem. Since fleas are pretty active and mobile, it is not likely that this tool will be of much help until the fleas have been killed or immobilized with a spray or dip.

GROOMING
TOOLS

pin brush

slicker brush

flea comb

towel

mat rake

grooming glove

scissors

nail clippers

tooth-cleaning equipment

shampoo

conditioner

clippers

No clipping is required with Beagles, but show Beagles are trimmed with scissors and thinning shears when excess hair detracts from the clean lines so desirable in a show dog. The whiskers are usually trimmed for show, but a field trial beagler wouldn't think of tampering with any of his hound's sensory devices. Hounds shown at the Peterborough Hound Show in England or the Bryn Mawr Hound Show in the United States are shown in a natural state, with no trimming or other modifying techniques allowed.

Nails Need Trimming

If your Beagle spends a lot of time exercising, or is kept part-time in a gravel or concrete run, her nails may not require much attention, but in most cases, you can expect to trim your Beagle's nails as needed. If you begin doing this when your puppy is small, it should never become the ordeal it seems to be for some people—sometimes requiring the vet to cut them!

After trimming your Beagle's nails, you can use a grinder to smooth them down.

Begin trimming nails when your puppy can be held easily under one arm and therefore be less mobile than if on a table. On a young puppy, a human-type fingernail clipper will work; then later you can switch to the kinds sold in pet shops. These are relatively inexpensive, so it often pays to buy the top-quality model. I prefer the single-blade models, but others are equally devoted to the type with two cutting blades, so you decide. But do buy one and use it regularly, and save the vet for more important functions. If you begin when your hound is young, you will better be able to see the "quick," or the blood supply to the nail, as the nails are more transparent in puppies.

Don't panic if you accidentally cut the nail too short. Just apply a little pressure or styptic powder, and keep the pup immobilized until the bleeding stops. I have never heard of a puppy bleeding to death from a trimming mistake, but I have heard of hounds whose feet were ruined by lack of trimming, so incompetence is better than neglect.

Electric nail files are available for people who want the perfect canine pedicure, but unless you are serious about showing, these are not necessary. If you do wish to smooth out the nail after clipping, a medium-coarse wood file will do the job.

Keep Those Ears Clean

The Beagle's ears require regular monitoring, and regular cleaning will help prevent things like ear mites, canker or ear infections. Breeds with pendulous ears are more prone to ear problems, so here a bit of routine maintenance is in order. About once a month, put a drop or two of plain mineral oil in each ear and, with your thumb and forefinger, gently massage the ear at its base, nearest the skull, until you hear a squishing sound. Then, using a cotton ball, gently swab out the ear, taking care not to delve too deeply into the ear canal. This procedure should take only a few minutes if done regularly, and if it helps you avoid ear problems, it is well worth it.

Tooth Care

More and more research is being done which suggests that dental care is more than just an aesthetic issue. In the past, people gave dogs bones, and there is no doubt that chewing bones is the most natural and effective method of preventing or removing dental calculus (tartar). One unfortunate side effect to this method, however, is the occasional accidental lodging of these bones in the mouth or throat, or in rare cases irritation or puncture of the digestive system. For this reason, this practice has long been discouraged by the veterinary profession.

You'll want to check your Beagle's teeth regularly to make sure tartar isn't building up and the gums are healthy.

Substitute bones like biscuits, chew toys or treats are not nearly as effective, but they are safer. Many vets also are advising pet owners to brush their pet's teeth and use the canine equivalent of floss. If you subscribe to this practice, begin doing it when your puppy is young and impressionable; otherwise it will be an ordeal.

Calculus left unchecked will eventually cause gum disease and tooth loss. There is also some evidence that

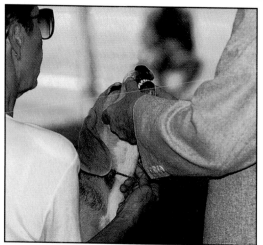

it will shorten your pet's life by contributing to kidney disease. Your vet can advise on the best ways to prevent this buildup and can also clean your hound's teeth for you, but as this can be a fairly expensive procedure, you will want to learn all you can do to prevent problems before they become serious.

In summary, the Beagle is one of the easiest breeds to keep well-groomed, and this grooming has numerous payoffs in areas other than the good looks of your pet. Instituted early and made a regular part of your interaction with your Beagle, grooming will extend the life and improve the quality of life of your best canine friend.

chapter 7

Keeping Your
Beagle
Healthy

As previously stated, the Beagle is a low-maintenance, remarkably hardy little hound, with a lusty appetite and variable activity level. He is also a typically carefree character not prone to the anxiety or neuroses seen in some breeds. All these things contribute to the basic good health of the breed. Also, whereas congenital or hereditary diseases have plagued many breeds, the Beagle on the whole seems to have gotten off pretty lightly. If you are conscientious about your

pet's feeding and grooming, and provide him with regular veterinary tune-ups, he should live a long and happy life.

There are entire books written on the subject of dog health and disease (many are listed in Chapter 12, "Recommended Reading"), and a number of maladies and accidental injuries are described here. Dog owners, however, should keep in mind that—as is also the case with the human species—just because there are a million diseases a dog can get, it doesn't mean he will get them!

The parts of this chapter you should take very seriously are those that deal with preventing diseases and accidents and developing a long-term working relationship with your veterinarian. As for the rest, read carefully, store it all in the back of your mind, but don't worry!

Choosing Your Vet

You should select a veterinarian with the same kind of care you take in selecting your family physician. There is tremendous variation among vets in treatment philosophy, specialization and fee schedules. Also, the personality of the vet is important. Is he or she someone you can feel comfortable talking to, or do you feel rushed during your visits? Are things explained to you in advance, or do you feel left in the dark? Are the routine visits costing you more than a comparable trip to a neurosurgeon? All these things contribute to how effective your relationship will be with your Beagle's vet, and so they deserve your attention.

Your Beagle requires regular "maintenance" by a vet, and any of the aforementioned factors that work to keep you away from his or her office are consequently bad for your pet. I recommend asking your puppy's breeder for a referral, then branching out to other dog-owning friends or even your local animal shelter. When you have narrowed down your choices, speak to the vets on the phone.

> ### YOUR PUPPY'S VACCINES
>
> Vaccines are given to prevent your dog from getting an infectious disease like canine distemper or rabies. Vaccines are the ultimate preventive medicine: they're given before your dog ever gets the disease so as to protect him from the disease. That's why it is necessary for your dog to be vaccinated routinely. Puppy vaccines start at eight weeks of age for the five-in-one DHLPP vaccine and are given every three to four weeks until the puppy is sixteen months old. Your veterinarian will put your puppy on a proper schedule and will remind you when to bring in your dog for shots.

Ask what constitutes "routine care" and what it will cost
you for the year. Most veterinarians have computerized
billing now, so they have a very clear idea what you will
pay. These questions are very reasonable, yet few people ask them ahead of time. Obviously, money should
not be the only factor in the decision process, but, on
the other hand, I would be reluctant to deal with someone who seems offended or intentionally vague when
that subject is raised.

I have been fortunate over the years to have worked
with some wonderful vets who have increased my
knowledge of dogs and the ways in which to keep them
healthy. With luck, and a little homework, I'm sure you
will, too.

Vaccines

Most people, even if they have never owned a dog,
have a vague notion of a puppy needing "shots." Think
of the immunizations you have had in your lifetime.
Beginning in childhood, you have been immunologi-
cally protected from every disease for which a practical, effective and safe vaccine exists. This is what we
attempt to do with our little hounds, and there is cause
to hope that the number of preventable diseases will
increase with the increasing knowledge of the immune
system and new breakthroughs in biotechnology.

When one reads of the kennels of yesteryear and how
distemper wiped out half the puppies each season, it is
hard to imagine why anyone today would not take
advantage of all the peace of mind that modern vaccination affords.

How Vaccination Works

Vaccination is the process of encouraging the immune
system to produce antibodies against certain diseases,
and usually this is done by injecting a weakened (atten-
uated or modified-live) or killed form of the organism
against which you want to immunize. Antibodies are
also passed on to puppies by their dams, and this is why
vaccination seldom is undertaken prior to weaning. In

65

fact, these so-called maternal antibodies may block the
effects of vaccination and prevent the puppy from
developing his own active immunity. For this reason,
vaccination begins as soon as puppies are weaned, and
it continues at regular intervals until the average age
when maternal antibodies are completely gone.

When parvovirus was new, many puppies died because
the shots stopped before the puppy was old enough

*If you keep your
puppy or dog
on a regular
vaccination
schedule, you
can almost
ensure she
won't get many
diseases.*

to develop his own active immunity. Today, it is believed that this
age is between fourteen to six-
teen weeks. So, when your vet has
you coming back for "puppy
shots" every two weeks, there
is a good reason. Vaccination
failure—when an animal falls ill
from a disease already vaccinated
against—is usually the result of
unlucky timing rather than any
problem with the vaccine. Later,
we will look at the diseases for
which we vaccinate, but this
explains the process and the
need for repeated vaccinations.
Once the initial immunization
has been completed, annual boosters are required to
maintain the protection.

Worming

In the case of worming, with the exception of heartworm prevention, the task is to detect the presence of
internal parasites before they have an opportunity to
cause clinical disease, to select the least toxic and most
effective medication to eliminate them, and then take
whatever steps possible to prevent reinfection.

In most cases the breeder would have been sure that
the dam was as free of parasites as possible, and that
the puppies were wormed at least twice prior to weaning. You should still bring a stool sample to the vet for

your puppy's first visit. It is considerably easier to keep one puppy worm-free in a pet situation than to do the same for several puppies in a kennel.

Bringing in a stool sample for each subsequent visit (with your veterinarian's approval) will help determine how successful you have been in eliminating the parasites. Picking up stools frequently and keeping the Beagle's living area clean will help prevent reinfection.

Now that we have looked at the reasons for worming and vaccinating, let us look at the diseases and worms we are concerned with.

Internal Parasites

What we commonly call worms are parasites ranging in size from less than an inch to several feet long. They may be nothing more than a nuisance in some cases or can be life-threatening in others. Generally speaking, puppies or weak animals are more susceptible to parasitic disease, and it is better to prevent or treat early than to wait until the puppy is weakened. A number of internal parasites may infect dogs, but the most common are roundworms, hookworms, tapeworms and whipworms.

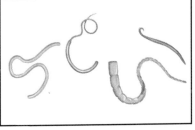

Roundworms (Ascarids) are present in all newborn puppies, regardless of whether the dam was wormed before or even during the pregnancy. About six inches long and the thickness of a pencil lead, they quickly lead to the debilitation or death of a Beagle puppy when their numbers increase. A puppy with an infestation of roundworms will typically have a dull coat, foul "sweet-smelling" breath, and a pot-bellied appearance. Roundworms can cause diarrhea, coughing, and vomiting, and what is called verminous pneumonia, which can open the way for secondary bacterial infections.

Common internal parasites (l-r): roundworm, whipworm, tapeworm and hookworm.

The good news is that while not preventable, round-worms are easily treated if detected early.

Hookworms are small (one-half inch) worms that attach themselves to the intestinal walls and suck blood. Not all puppies are born with hookworms, as is the case with roundworms, but most "puppy wormers" are effective against both, so if the breeder was on top of things, you shouldn't have to be concerned with hookworm disease. A puppy with hookworm disease will have the poor coat of the roundworm puppy, but also will show signs of anemia (pale gums) and have bloody or tarry stools. Both roundworms and hook-worms can cause clinical disease in humans, so that is even more reason to keep your pet worm-free.

Tapeworms are the largest internal parasite but, iron-ically, the least harmful to its host. Tapeworm infection requires an intermediate host, the most common type being carried by the flea. Another is the type caused by the ingestion of dead rodents or rabbits, a problem for some hunting Beagles.

The most obvious sign that your pet has tapeworms is the presence of segments in the stool. These segments are flat and up to one-half inch long, and may be mov-ing when evacuated. They may be seen near the anus of the dog and when dried out appear more rice-like. Occasionally, having tapeworms may cause the dog to "scoot," or drag his hind end on the ground (more commonly, however, this behavior is caused by impacted anal glands). In order to treat tapeworms successfully, you must eliminate the fleas, as well. The medications available today for treating tapeworms are far safer and easier to use than their predecessors, without the fasting and mess.

Whipworms are small, threadlike worms (two inches long) that resemble miniature whips, hence the name. Since they set up housekeeping in the cecum, or "blind gut," they are harder to treat than worms in the rest of the digestive system. Whipworms are hard to eradicate from the kennel as well, so prevention is important.

Symptoms of whipworm disease include weight loss, poor coat and loose stools, often containing mucus. Dogs can have a light infection and not show symptoms, only to have a flare-up if subjected to stress. For this reason, plus the fact that whipworms lay eggs sporadically, whipworm may be hard to diagnose.

Heartworms differ from other internal parasites of dogs in that they infect the circulatory system as opposed to the digestive system. Spread by mosquitoes, this parasite, once seen only in the southern states, is a problem all over the country. Part of your pet's routine maintenance will be an annual test for the presence of these silent killers prior to putting him on preventive medication.

With new medications that need be administered only once a month and which often help control other parasites as well, this disease is easily prevented. Cure for the infected dog is another matter. Since the worms, often up to twelve inches in length, cluster and inhabit the circulatory system, primarily the heart, too abrupt a death of these creatures can cause severe blockage and death. Also, the agents used to kill the worms are in themselves fairly toxic, so the need to avoid these threats to your Beagle's life is of prime importance.

FIGHTING FLEAS

Remember, the fleas you see on your dog are only part of the problem—the smallest part! To rid your dog and home of fleas, you need to treat your dog *and* your home. Here's how:

• Identify where your pets sleep. These are "hot spots."

• Clean your pets' bedding regularly by vacuuming and washing.

• Spray "hot spots" with a nontoxic, long-lasting flea larvicide.

• Treat outdoor "hot spots" with insecticide.

• Kill eggs on pets with a product containing insect growth regulators (IGRs).

• Kill fleas on pets per your veterinarian's recommendation.

Symptoms of heartworm disease vary according to the primary site of the infestation, but the most common symptom is a quiet, non-productive cough and lack of energy. In hunting Beagles, an otherwise fit hound will tire easily and appear weakened. Actual heartworm disease may take more than a year to develop after the dog has been infected as the maturation and migration of the parasite takes place, so by the time the animal shows clinical signs of heartworm, the infection is fairly advanced. Again, this means that testing and keeping up the preventive medication is important.

External Parasites

These are the next most common causes of complaint among dog owners, and once again, Beagles are not exempt. The most frequently found external parasites are fleas, ticks and mites. Lice are rarely a problem.

Fleas have always been with us, and with their ability to reproduce rapidly and develop resistance to various insecticides, there is a good chance they will always be with us. The thing that is perplexing about fleas is the

The flea is a die-hard pest.

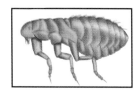

way different animals react to their presence. Some dogs can have a sizeable population of fleas on them and not react, and others can have one or two and tear themselves to shreds chewing and scratching at them. This latter phenomenon can confound pet owners who can't see any fleas but only the aftereffects of the scratching and chewing, causing them to believe that the cause of the skin disorder must be something other than fleas.

Many years ago I used a veterinary practice that employed a canine dermatologist who confided in me that a majority of the cases he treated were flea-related. When you add to this the fact that the common tapeworm is transmitted by fleas, the need to eliminate fleas is apparent. Since the flea lives both on the host or in its environment (deep carpeting is a favorite), successful treatment involves treating both the pet and the living area.

Repeated treatments are usually necessary, since most products used kill only the adult fleas. The key, then, is to interrupt the reproductive cycle by killing the young adult fleas before they reproduce. In some cases, your vet may prescribe a treatment whose mode of action involves preventing the immature stages from maturing. Whatever you do, treat fleas seriously. In kennel situations, they are a constant nuisance, and in the house, with endless hiding places and the inability to hose things down and disinfect, the problem is equally serious. Do not try to treat the situation in a hit-or-miss fashion. Consult your vet and do what you have to do to eliminate them from your pet's environment. Remember, if you just knock them down or reduce their numbers, the survivors and their offspring are likely to be more resistant to subsequent treatments.

Ticks are the next most common external parasite of dogs, and whereas the major risk in the past was debilitation due to heavy infestations both from the blood loss and the toxins secreted by the ticks themselves, ticks have

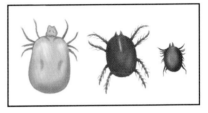

always been capable of transmitting serious diseases. While everyone today has heard about Lyme disease, ironically, this may soon be the least of our worries as it relates to our Beagles. A vaccine is currently available in states with the highest incidence of Lyme disease, so soon we may have to worry only about diseases like Rocky Mountain spotted fever, tularemia, and encephalitis.

Three types of ticks (l-r): the wood tick, brown dog tick and deer tick.

In other words, ticks will always be a source of concern for us as beaglers and pet owners. The aforementioned diseases are potentially fatal to humans, so in addition to keeping ticks off our pets, we need to check ourselves after potential exposure. It is not necessary to be in the country to be exposed to ticks—they live as happily in suburban or urban parks as in farm fields.

The most common tick is the dog tick, but there are many other varieties and none of them are beneficial, so there is no real need to distinguish them. Presently it is believed that the tiny deer tick is the primary carrier of Lyme disease, but it is being transmitted by the dog tick as well. Your vet can advise you on the best prevention for ticks, but once you see one on yourself or your pet, remove it at once. Use a pair of tweezers and apply steady, twisting traction to remove it, head and all. A drop of alcohol may encourage the pest to release its grip, but if the head remains, don't worry.

Check your Beagle after each trip afield and remove the little menaces before they have a chance to attach

themselves and transmit disease. Current Lyme disease research suggests that it may take up to forty-eight hours for an infected tick to transmit the disease, so with vigilance and frequent grooming, as well as the availability of vaccines and repellents, pet owners have no good reason to remain inside a bubble!

Mites are another ubiquitous problem for our hounds and come in a number of different types. Ear mites are probably present in most mature Beagles kept in kennels. Why they become a problem for some hounds

Use tweezers to remove ticks from your dog.

and not others is a mystery, but when they cause a clinical infection, they make a hound miserable. The hound thus afflicted will scratch at the inside of her ear and constantly shake her head.

The pet who has her ears cleaned regularly should never develop this problem, and this is yet another example of an ounce of prevention being worth a pound of slow and tedious cure. The mineral oil or oily cleaning solution will usually control light infections by cutting off the pest's oxygen supply, but once a serious infection has developed, not only do we have to worry about the mites but we have to be concerned with secondary bacterial or fungal infections. Your vet will check your hound's ears as part of her regular checkup. That is a good time to learn how to do a thorough cleaning for your hound's regular grooming routine.

Mange mites come in two major types.

Demodectic mange, either in its localized or generalized form, has been considered as much a problem with the animal's immune system as with the mere presence of

72

mites. The mite that causes this disease is present in all dogs, yet only a few will develop the symptoms, which include hair loss without itching, and a "moth-eaten" look. The number of lesions present determine whether the condition is termed localized or generalized. This disease is seen mostly in young puppies but can occur in older, stressed individuals. Contagion is rarely a problem. Demodectic mange is much less responsive to insecticidal dips than is sarcoptic mange, and many "cures" are probably attributable to raising the animal's nutritional level and the subsequent boostering of its immune response, as much as the actual treatment. It is likely that some animals have a genetic predisposition to this affliction, and for that reason, Beagles from families where this has been a problem should not be bred.

Sarcoptic mange, unlike demodectic mange, is highly contagious and causes intense itching. The same mite causes scabies in humans—the infection is similar in the way the mite burrows under the skin—and in fact we can contract the mite from our pets. The skin of the dog will become reddened, then crusty as the itching causes the dog to self-mutilate.

The good news about this condition is that it is highly responsive to simple insecticidal treatment, and your vet should be able to clean things up in short order. Be sure to thoroughly clean and disinfect the pet's living area after treatment.

Ringworm is not caused by a worm or mite, but I include it here because it is another common skin infection in Beagles and it may be confused with parasitic disease. Ringworm, named after the ring-like lesions it produces, is actually caused by a fungus. It causes hair loss and itching, and can be contagious to other animals and to humans.

While skin scrapings are necessary for detecting the presence of mites, a Wood's lamp, a specialized kind of blacklight, will cause the spores that cause ringworm to fluoresce. If your pet has only a couple of lesions, your vet may have you treat him topically, taking care not to infect yourself in the process, but in some cases, a systemic fungicide may be used.

"Hot Spots" are different from all of the preceding afflictions because they appear almost overnight and cause instant hair loss and itching. The resulting lesion is raw-looking and moist. The causes of this condition are unclear, but treatment usually involves anti-inflammatory agents to reduce the itching and thereby prevent further skin damage or secondary infection.

For years beaglers have used home remedies to treat these various problems, but I won't perpetuate this practice by repeating them here. Some of them worked reasonably well in the absence of more specific medications, but in many cases the "cure" was more likely the result of the condition being self-limiting. You and your pet are best served by having these conditions diagnosed and treated by your veterinarian.

Common Canine Diseases

As promised, here are the most common canine diseases, almost all of which are preventable with regular vaccinations.

Distemper was the major killer of puppies in the Beagle kennels of old, often eliminating entire litters of puppies. A viral disease with a number of different forms, the most common involves severe respiratory infection resembling a "cold," progressing to neurological involvement and usually death. There is no drug to kill the virus, and even if a puppy survives, he will likely be permanently impaired, so prevention is the key. The distemper virus is ever-present, and the fact that we don't hear much about it is a testimony to modern veterinary medicine and the effectiveness of present-day vaccines.

Hepatitis is a viral infection that attacks the liver and kidney, progresses rapidly and is highly contagious. It causes acute diarrhea, usually bloody, and is accompanied by high fever. Treatment is supportive and symptomatic, but again, as it is a virus, there is no cure. It is one of the diseases included in most multivalent vaccines, so when your puppy or adult hound gets either puppy shots or annual boosters, you can be reasonably sure that she is being protected against hepatitis.

Leptospirosis is a disease that damages the liver and kidneys and is transmitted in the urine, primarily by rats. Caused by a spirochete (the same type of organism that causes Lyme disease and syphilis), this disease is treatable. However, as it is easily preventable through vaccination and because it poses a risk to humans, prevention should be a priority.

The kidney and liver damage associated with severe cases of leptospirosis cause a complex of symptoms beginning with depression, anorexia and fever, and progressing to vomiting and diarrhea. The afflicted animal will have increased thirst and may be reluctant to leave a sitting position due to the internal pain associated with the infection. Body temperature will drop, and lesions resembling burns will appear on the tongue and gums. The eyes, which initially may have appeared reddish, then acquire a yellowish cast associated with liver disease. Mortality may be around 10 percent, but treated animals may remain carriers.

Keeping fleas and ticks off your Beagles is a constant job, but one well worth doing. Your hounds, home and yard may need treatment.

Tracheobronchitis is the official name for a complex of organisms that cause what is commonly known as *kennel cough*. Spread in boarding kennels or contracted at shows or field trials, it is highly contagious, but in most cases only a nuisance. The afflicted dog will have a hacking cough and occasionally spit up a foamy sputum. In most cases the dog will continue to eat normally and the disease will be self-limiting. Occasionally, however, secondary bacterial infections may set in and will require antibiotic therapy.

Living with a
Beagle

Many multivalent vaccines contain fractions for kennel cough, and there are separate vaccines specifically for other agents that cause the disease, but since there are many more types of kennel cough than there are vaccines, complete protection is impossible. The best one can do is to vaccinate for what is preventable, avoid situations where exposure is likely, and be in touch with your vet if all these measures fail. The course of this illness is one to two weeks, and should it last any longer, other complications should be suspected. If the persistent coughing is bothering you or your pet excessively, your vet may prescribe an expectorant cough syrup to help alleviate the symptoms.

WHEN TO CALL THE VET

In any emergency situation, you should call your veterinarian immediately. You can make the difference in your dog's life by staying as calm as possible when you call and by giving the doctor or the assistant as much information as possible before you leave for the clinic. That way, the vet will be able to take immediate, specific action to remedy your dog's situation.

Emergencies include acute abdominal pain, suspected poisoning, snakebite, burns, frostbite, shock, dehydration, abnormal vomiting or bleeding, and deep wounds. You are the best judge of your dog's health, as you live with and observe him every day. Don't hesitate to call your veterinarian if you suspect trouble.

Parvovirus and **Coronavirus** are two viral enteric diseases that may be deadly to puppies or young hounds. A puppy healthy and frisky one day can be dead the next morning if struck by some of the more virulent forms of these diseases. Vomiting and diarrhea are the two most prevalent symptoms, including bloody diarrhea.

I had the misfortune of losing several hounds to parvo when it first surfaced as a "new" disease in the early 1980s. There was no vaccine available, and since it was new there were no protective antibodies in the canine population. After an experience like that, one never takes shortcuts in the vaccination program!

Vaccines are available for these two diseases, though coronavirus is seldom included in multivalent vaccines. Be sure to consult with your vet on the most foolproof way to prevent these deadly diseases. It is practically impossible to overvaccinate, but a lapse in your puppy's antibodies at the wrong time could be disastrous. Older animals may contract either of these diseases and recover with appropriate treatment such as fluid replacement therapy, but there is evidence that these viruses are capable of mutating to more virulent forms, so it is best to keep the vaccinations up to date rather than take any risks.

If I seem to be constantly repeating the message that annual boosters are necessary, it is because you will likely encounter well-meaning "experts" who will tell you that your hound doesn't need all those shots, and that after the puppy series he should be set for life. They may even offer their own experience as evidence that their hound or hounds have done well without boosters.

When you hear this, remember that there are also people who can drive fast and violate traffic laws for extended periods of time without anything bad happening to them. What we are talking about here is a type of reverse lottery with the "jackpot" being more grief than anyone needs. Vaccination is cheap insurance—don't gamble with your pet's health.

Rabies is the only disease your dog must be vaccinated against as far as the law is concerned. This is because of the very real threat of a human contracting the fatal disease from a rabid dog. This law has been so successful that the number of cases where a human has been exposed by a dog is extremely low. Because of this, however, people tend to be complacent or to think that rabies is a thing of the past. Nothing could be further from the truth.

In recent years, rabies has appeared in areas that hadn't seen it in many years. Occurring mostly in nocturnal animals like bats, raccoons and skunks, this disease can infect any warm-blooded animal. Any otherwise nocturnal animal seen wandering around during the day should be suspect. Also, remember that many communities lack the resources to ensure that cats be licensed and vaccinated, and since many of these animals are allowed to roam at will, their risk of exposure is greater than that of the average house dog.

Living with a
Beagle

If a human is exposed, the treatment is a series of shots to confer immunity before the disease takes hold. Once the symptoms appear, it is too late. Most vaccines for rabies are effective for three years, but if your Beagle is going to be allowed to hunt (thereby increasing his risk of exposure), you may want to ask your vet about annual vaccination. Most people's perception of rabies involves a "mad dog" foaming at the mouth, but the disease can take a very different "dumb" form as well as the furious form. Encephalitis is common to both forms, and paralysis and death follow within ten days of the appearance of the first symptoms.

If your pet is exposed to a possibly rabid animal and is not current in his vaccination, your choice is generally either to destroy him or place him in a veterinary-supervised quarantine for up to four months. This is why regular vaccination is such a good idea.

Inherited Diseases of Beagles

As noted at the beginning of this chapter, there are few problems that are unique to Beagles as a breed, but some things afflict Beagles more than other breeds, and some conditions which may not effect the whole breed may occur in certain strains or families.

Epilepsy is a case in point, and while not hereditary, strictly speaking, it does appear in some families more than in others. The degree of severity can range from the *petit mal* form, which may appear to be nothing more than the dog "spacing out" for a few minutes, to *grand mal*, which involves loss of muscular control, stiffening and convulsing. The latter, often terrifying to the owner, may last several minutes, during which time you are convinced your dog is going to die. The dog then acts subdued or disoriented for a few more minutes and then acts as if nothing ever happened.

Closely related is another condition in Beagles known as "running fits," which occur when the hound is hunting and suddenly runs off as if being chased by the devil himself! A number of theories have been posited concerning this condition, including internal

78

parasites, nutritional deficiencies, or low blood sugar, but it remains a mystery.

In the case of epilepsy, mild forms present no major problems for the average house pet, but the more serious forms will no doubt require medication, as in the case of human epilepsy. Needless to say, an epileptic animal should never be bred.

Cherry Eye, or the infection and swelling of the third eyelid, is common in Beagles and may be treated with a simple surgical procedure or may even respond to antibiotics. The condition looks a lot worse than it is, since the swelling and redness are prominent, but many animals don't seem to know there is any problem. This problem should be distinguished from conjunctivitis, excessive tear production, corneal abrasions or a more serious condition known as dry eyes.

Back or disc problems occur occasionally in Beagles, but a Beagle with correct conformation kept in fit condition will be far less likely to have problems than will a long-bodied or sway-backed Beagle carrying excessive weight. Treatment varies in type and in degree of success, so selection of a sound puppy from correctly built parents is the best form of prevention. Breeders could go a long way towards eliminating this condition by breeding older, sound animals with no history of back problems, since it rarely occurs in younger animals. In some cases, rest followed by moderate exercise will be

IDENTIFYING YOUR DOG

It's a terrible thing to think about, but your dog could somehow, someday, get lost or stolen. How would you get him back? Your best bet would be to have some form of identification on your dog. You can choose from a collar and tags, a tattoo, a microchip or a combination of these three.

Every dog should wear a buckle collar with identification tags. They are the quickest and easiest way for a stranger to identify your dog. It's best to inscribe the tags with your name and phone number; you don't need to include your dog's name.

There are two ways to permanently identify your dog. The first is a tattoo, placed on the inside of your dog's thigh. The tattoo should be your social security number or your dog's AKC registration number.

The second is a microchip, a rice-sized pellet that's inserted under the dog's skin at the base of the neck, between the shoulder blades. When a scanner is passed over the dog, it will beep, notifying the person that the dog has a chip. The scanner will then show a code, identifying the dog. Microchips are becoming more and more popular and are certainly the wave of the future.

enough to bring relief, but in more severe cases anti-inflammatory drugs or even surgery may be required.

Preventive Care

As we have said, the Beagle is a remarkably hardy little creature and with good care should remain healthy most of the time. Now let us look more critically at the preventive components of feeding, grooming and housing.

Feeding is the cornerstone of a sound health care program for your Beagle. The old Irish admonition that hounds should be "fed hungry" should be your guide to feeding your Beagle. If you overfeed, you lose one of the best diagnostic indicators as to your hound's health. When you limit-feed your hound and feed the same food consistently, he should approach his bowl with gusto. If, on the other hand, you have been switching foods or overindulging him with table scraps, you will not know whether he is "off his feed" because of illness or because he is full, or spoiled.

If your Beagle seems "off" in any way—if she's sleeping too much, for example—it could be a sign that something's wrong.

Many foods so beloved by us are threatening to your Beagle's health. For example, highly spiced foods may cause intestinal upset, diarrhea, or, in extreme cases, seizures. Chocolate is toxic to all dogs, and while there may be no cause for panic if your pet steals the occasional chocolate chip cookie, he should definitely be

watched carefully after accidental (on your part) ingestion of large amounts of chocolate. A more unusual
food poisoning may occur if your pet eats raw onions,
which are toxic to dogs.

It was already noted in Chapter 5 that a good-quality,
nutrient-dense dry food is all your pet needs, but many
people succumb to the urge to "pamper" their hound
by cooking for her or regularly adding supplements
to her diet. This is not only unnecessary and a waste
of your time and money, but may be harmful to your
pet's health.

For example, it was common practice for years for people to add a raw egg to their dog's food "for the coat."
It turns out, however, that the uncooked egg white
actually interferes with the dog's ability to digest an
important amino acid. Cooked eggs are a high-quality
food, but, again, unless you are feeding a sick animal,
no special meals should be necessary.

The last word on feeding is some necessary discussion
of the food's inevitable by-product, the stool. A good
veterinary diagnostician can tell a great deal about the
health of an animal from its stool. We, on the other
hand, are inclined not to look too closely and to dispose of things as quickly as possible. The configuration
of your dog's stool will give you important clues concerning whether she is properly digesting the food you
are providing, whether you may be overfeeding, or
whether she has been getting into something bad for
her. A sudden change from a firm, well-formed stool to
something loose or runny should be a warning sign.

Diarrhea by itself is a symptom rather than a separate
illness and may be treated symptomatically, but
remember that the cause must be addressed as well.
Human medications like Pepto Bismol or Kaopectate
may be used to arrest the symptomatic diarrhea, and
hamburger and boiled rice may be substituted for your
hound's regular diet until things have calmed down.

A stool that is hard and dry may signal that your pet
isn't getting enough water or fiber. Finally, a regular

visual assessment of the stool will give you some idea as to the potential presence of internal parasites. Roundworms and tapeworm segments are easily seen in the stool (although their absence in the stool does not mean your pet is parasite-free), but the presence of other parasites may be inferred if you see mucus or blood in the stool. That is your cue to get a sample off to your vet for microscopic examination.

Grooming, in addition to keeping your Beagle looking good and improving the human-canine bond, will give you ample opportunity to check your pet for external parasites or any developing skin problems. You will regularly be cleaning your Beagle's ears, trimming his nails (including the dewclaws on the inside of the front legs), and cleaning his teeth as instructed by your vet. If you have been doing this for

Check your dog's teeth frequently and brush them regularly.

your hound since puppyhood, he should be easy to work with and won't flinch or panic when your vet has to work with him.

Ask your veterinarian whether your pet will ever need to have his **anal glands** emptied. These glands are located on either side of the anus and are related to the scent glands on skunks and foxes. If your pet has ever been badly frightened and you have noted an unpleasant, "doggy" odor, it is because these glands have emptied. Normal, healthy dogs who get regular exercise and have normal, firm stools shouldn't have a problem. Obese dogs or dogs who produce loose stools are more likely to need to have these sacs emptied. If your pet is licking or biting at the anal region, or "scooting" (dragging his hindquarters along the ground), he may require attention. Of course, it goes without saying that once the symptom is alleviated, the underlying causes (incorrect diet, obesity) should be addressed.

If you hunt your Beagle, one further component of grooming involves checking your pet over when you get home. Weed seeds or other foreign objects can find their way into the eyes, and flushing with water or saline solution will reduce irritation. A good brushing will help locate and dislodge any burrs or thorns that may have found their way into the skin and which could be irritating.

Lameness, or the tendency to carry one foot off the ground, can be the result of any number of things, but it is best to start with the simplest causes first before panicking. If your hound has been afield, the most common culprit is an embedded thorn in the foot. It is often easiest to "feel" for these with your fingers, as there may be very little material sticking out. Minor lacerations usually don't require any treatment.

If the foot shows any redness or swelling, your Beagle may have an interdigital cyst and will require antibiotic therapy. If the foot is not the cause of the lameness, there could be a problem with the knee or stifle joint, or he may have bruised, twisted or otherwise made some part of the running gear tender. Since they are perfectly capable of motoring along just fine on three limbs, they often don't seem too upset when carrying one foot up. If the condition persists, however, it should be checked out.

This condition is very different from the one in which the hound suddenly develops a stiff gait or a hunched appearance. This may signify any number of things, none of them good, so a trip to the vet would be in order.

Lyme disease, disc problems, and kidney and enteric disease may all start like this, so don't delay professional diagnosis and treatment.

Taking Your Beagle's Temperature

Learn to take your pet's temperature. An elevated or depressed temperature may spell the difference between your hound just being "off his feed" for a day or the presence of some infection, which could be best treated early. Today we have digital thermometers that give a read-out in a matter of seconds, so taking your pet's temperature is not as big a project as it was when you had to wait a few minutes.

Ask someone to restrain the front end of your hound while you focus your attention on the other end. Grasp the base of the tail firmly, and with the other hand carefully insert a well-lubricated (with petroleum jelly) rectal thermometer into the anus. Holding your pet in this fashion should keep him fairly well immobilized. Be sure the thermometer you use is strong enough for this purpose; human oral-type thermometers are too fragile. The average temperature of the dog is approximately 101 degrees Fahrenheit, but there may be normal variation of a degree or so either way, so taking your pet's temperature before he is sick is a good way of establishing what his "baseline" is.

Medicating Your Beagle

If your vet sends you home with medication for your pet for whatever reason, have him or her demonstrate

how to administer it. I will explain the various methods here, but a live demonstration is still the best way to learn how to do something like this.

First let me say that sometimes the easy way is the best way, and medicine often can be "hidden" in the food. Gelatin capsules can be opened and their contents sprinkled and mixed in the food if a little moisture and flavoring is included.

Squeeze eye ointment into the lower lid.

Whereas old wormers usually involved fasting, or giving football-sized pills, most modern anthelmintics can be mixed in the food. Similarly, antibiotics (assuming they don't require being administered on an empty stomach) can be given this way. Pills can be crushed between sheets of paper and turned into a mixable powder. If your pet is eating only one meal a day and the medication must be given more frequently, you can divide the meal up into equal portions and not have to worry about overfeeding.

If you have to give a pill with no tricks allowed, put your pet on a table to get her closer to your eye level and immobilize her somewhat. With one hand, grasp the upper part of the muzzle and open her mouth. If you intentionally put her lips between her teeth and your fingers, she will be more reluctant to close her mouth before you are ready. With your other hand, place the pill as far back on her tongue as possible, taking care not to let it fall off to the side, where it may be bitten or expelled rather than swallowed. Close her mouth and hold her muzzle upright while stroking her throat to encourage swallowing. Keep doing this until you are sure she has swallowed. If your pet spits the pill out, keep at it until you succeed. You have to get the point across that you don't enjoy this any more than she does, but it has to be done!

To give a pill, open the mouth wide, then drop it in the back of the throat.

Liquid medications are pretty rare these days, and if you can't add it to the feed, ask your vet for a syringe (minus the needle). This is a much more controlled method of administering liquids than spoons, but the principle is the same. Here you want to keep her mouth closed, only opening the lips at the corner of her mouth. You then inject or pour the liquid in as you tilt the head back slightly. And you keep the muzzle closed until she swallows.

When to Call the Vet

The most common complaint I hear from vets is that people sometimes wait until too late to bring a sick animal in for treatment. No vet likes to lose a pet when timely treatment would have ensured a more positive outcome. The flip side of this coin is that many people feel stupid rushing to the vet for every little thing, especially if they are the kind who rarely seek out a doctor if they themselves are sick.

If you have developed a working relationship with your vet and he or she knows you and your Beagle, this decision will be easier. For one thing, you should have telephone access to your vet rather than having to speak through an intermediary, and he or she can help you decide over the phone whether immediate attention is required or whether you can be doing anything at home to either remedy the problem or help the vet better diagnose the situation. For example, if your hound suddenly goes off feed and doesn't want to leave his bed, your vet may ask you to take his temperature or answer other questions that will aid in his or her diagnosis. Even if you end up taking your Beagle to the vet, the phone call will speed things up on the other end since they will know what to expect when you arrive.

A FIRST-AID KIT

Keep a canine first-aid kit on hand for general care and emergencies. Check it periodically to make sure liquids haven't spilled or dried up, and replace medications and materials after they're used. Your kit should include:

Activated charcoal tablets

Adhesive tape
(1 and 2 inches wide)

Antibacterial ointment
(for skin and eyes)

Aspirin (buffered or enteric coated, *not* ibuprofen)

Bandages: Gauze rolls (1 and 2 inches wide) and dressing pads

Cotton balls

Diarrhea medicine

Dosing syringe

Hydrogen peroxide (3%)

Petroleum jelly

Rectal thermometer

Rubber gloves

Rubbing alcohol

Scissors

Tourniquet

Towel

Tweezers

Signs of Sickness

The sorts of things that should cause you to consult your vet are sudden food refusal when accompanied by lethargy, vomiting or diarrhea, or elevated temperature. Also, any sudden tenderness or indication that your pet is in pain should be a red flag. Beagles are stoics, so if they show signs of being in pain, it is time to call the vet. Bloody stools are another indication that all is not well and deserve professional attention sooner rather than later.

Dehydration is another symptom that something is wrong, and it is important that you be able to recognize when your Beagle is dehydrated. To test for dehydration, lift the loose skin on the top of your hound's neck. It should return to its previous position almost immediately under normal conditions, but if he is dehydrated, the skin will return slowly, signalling a lack of fluid and plasticity. While dehydration is a symptom and not a disease, the electrolyte imbalances it causes can have serious consequences.

Vomiting is a symptom of many things as well, and while most of the time it signifies nothing serious, you should always make a note of the incident and begin to distinguish the causes and product of the vomiting. For example, a hacking cough followed by a "spitting up" of saliva could mean kennel cough, some type of worm infection, or just that your pet accidentally ingested a "dust kitty" from under the bed and is spitting it out. Similarly, if your puppy begins vigorous exercise after a big meal and regurgitates part of it, this is nor-

Applying abdominal thrusts can save a choking dog.

mal. It is also normal for them to then reingest this little mishap! However, if vomiting is accompanied by anorexia or elevated temperature, call your vet.

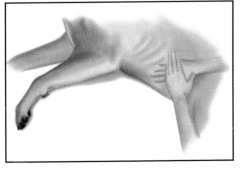

In the spring and summer, you will have a hard time dissuading your Beagle from eating the nice green grass. There are many theories about why they do this ("spring tonic" and so forth), but the inevitable result is the regurgitation of this crude salad. This is normal and harmless, though unpleasant.

Accidents, including those involving automobiles, generally warrant veterinary care even if the outward damage doesn't seem great at the time. Internal damage can be a silent killer, or your hound could go into shock. Call ahead to discuss what to do by way of alleviating your pet's distress and transporting him without exacerbating the problem. Typically, the procedure will be to keep the injured animal warm and quiet during transport, taking care to move him as little as possible.

If **bleeding** is involved, either direct pressure or a tourniquet may be employed, depending on the location of the wound. These are to be considered first-aid measures only, and you should waste no time getting professional help. If you use a tourniquet, remember to release pressure periodically so as not to cut off circulation for too long.

Make a temporary splint by wrapping the leg in firm casing, then bandaging it.

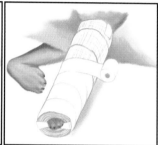

If your pet is badly injured, he is not going to react like himself, so you may need to muzzle him to prevent being bitten. Simply tying his muzzle shut with a strip of cloth will serve as an emergency muzzle, but if he shows no tendency to strike out, it is better to leave it off, since he may be having difficulty breathing already.

Use a scarf or old hose to make a temporary muzzle, as shown.

Poisonings

Accidental poisoning can have disastrous results, and prevention is the best course of action. A surprising array of seemingly harmless substances are toxic to dogs, in addition to the obvious suspects of pesticides and rodenticides. One of the most common forms of accidental poisoning in dogs is from ingesting ethylene glycol (**antifreeze**), which has an appealing taste to dogs and can cause death when relatively small amounts are consumed. New formulations of antifreeze are currently on the market that do not contain this chemical, and it would be prudent to use this type if you are likely to have these things around your garage.

A number of **houseplants** are toxic to dogs, and all should be kept out of reach. Puppies especially are vulnerable, due to their indiscriminate chewing and low body weight. Plants in the garden can be problematic as well, so for the sake of your puppy and your plants, keep them apart.

Accidental poisoning can occur when normally safe compounds are mixed together, as in the case of organophosphate poisoning. Certain wormers, when administered at the same time as certain **insecticides,** may have dire consequences. For this reason alone, it is unwise to use these products without veterinary supervision.

Some of the many household substances harmful to your dog.

Rat poisons vary in their mode of action, some requiring repeated feedings, and others only one dose. Many are blended with flavoring agents attractive to dogs as well as rodents, so if you must use them, keep them in pet-proof bait stations. If you suspect your pet has ingested rat poison, immediately call the 800 number on the package or the Poison Control center. They will be able to advise as to what course of action you or your vet should take.

Human painkillers can be toxic to dogs, and many dog owners who attempt to treat their pets with acetomeniphen or ibuprophen accidentally poison them. The confusion arises because aspirin has been used on horses and dogs for years with relative safety for arthritic conditions or as anti-inflammatory agents. This practice, or even the long-term use of a prescription anti-inflammatory, is of questionable merit and should be discussed candidly with your vet.

If your animal is in discomfort, rest is the best cure. If you repeatedly disguise the symptoms, you may be unintentionally exacerbating the underlying causes.

Heatstroke

Heatstroke can occur if your dog overexercises in the heat of the day, is left in a kennel with no shade or water, or, most commonly, is left in an improperly ventilated automobile in the sun. In the latter case, many people forget how quickly the interior of a car can heat up when the windows are shut. They think that leaving them open a crack (enough for fresh air) is suffi-

Run your hands regularly over your dog to feel for any injuries.

cient—after all, they reason, the Beagle might jump out the window. It can be heartbreaking to return from a relatively short shopping trip on a day only in the 70's to find your pet dead or in extreme distress from heat.

A dog suffering from heatstroke will have an elevated body temperature, will be panting loudly, and her tongue and gums will be bright red. Emergency treatment involves cooling her off as quickly as possible, including submerging her in cold water or administering a cold water enema. This latter procedure is to be left to your vet, but prompt action is required to reduce the animal's temperature before permanent damage occurs. Prevention, once again, is the watchword—and making sure that your pet is protected from extreme temperatures and always has plenty of cool, fresh water.

If you absolutely must travel with your Beagle in warm weather, consider using a wire crate and leaving the windows open. Park in the shade, and keep your errands brief.

Hunting Accidents

These come in all forms. Whether or not you personally are hunting, your Beagle may turn an exercise session into a sporting outing. It is not uncommon for them to get a bit scratched up in the briars, and a blood-tinged stern (tail) is a Beagle's badge of honor. When the end of the ear is nicked, however, they can often bleed enough to alarm their owners. A rabbit-hunting friend of mine had a hound whose ears bled easily, and he began carrying a few rubber bands in his pocket as emergency tourniquets! In most cases, it looks worse than it really is, but simple pressure will generally stop things quickly.

Encounters of Another Kind

More disconcerting is an accidental encounter with varmints like **skunks** or **porcupines.** In the latter case, these slow-moving denizens of the north woods can release hundreds of quills into an unsuspecting Beagle, generally in the face and mouth. This is a job for the vet, who may need to anaesthetize your pet before undertaking the painful and slow process. I have had Beagles quilled by dead porcupines who were interested in a bit of exotic carrion with a bite to it!

An Elizabethan collar keeps your dog from licking a fresh wound.

A skunk encounter is less painful but pretty unpleasant for the human. Actually, a direct hit in the eyes can burn your pet, but the sensation doesn't last long. The Beagle doesn't seem to mind the odor, which is somewhat surprising, considering his highly developed sense of smell. In fact, I once had an entire pack of young hounds sprayed up close, and the smell was almost palpable! I decided to keep them out a while longer to let them "air out" before returning to the kennel, and was astonished when they found the fresh track of the faint-smelling cottontail and ran it despite the overpowering skunk perfume!

The house pet thus afflicted will need a bath, then a soaking in tomato juice. There is a product out now specifically for skunk mishaps, but you are more likely to have easy access to tomato juice, and it works equally well.

At certain times of the year **ground wasps,** or **yellow jackets,** are in a mean mood, and if your pet bungles into their territory, he may be in for a rude shock. Also, if you try to rescue him and brush them off, you may be stung yourself. I have had this happen a number of times with no serious consequences, but years ago had a puppy go into anaphylactic shock after multiple stings. We have all heard of people dying from insect stings, and bee sting allergies seem to be on the rise, so watch your pet (and yourself) for reactions after these episodes.

Spaying and Neutering

With the serious problem of pet overpopulation in this country, there is no good reason for not surgically altering your pet unless you are competing in AKC field trials or shows, where spayed or neutered animals are not allowed to compete.

Many people are under the false impression that neutered animals get fat and lazy or are no longer useful for hunting, but there is no evidence that this is the case. In fact, hunters are generally pleased to no longer have to worry about losing three weeks during the rabbit season while their female is in heat.

The idea of having a litter of puppies to give children the experience of witnessing the "miracle of birth" is fortunately dying a natural death, and fewer people still believe that letting their bitch have just one litter would be "good for her." The mess and inconvenience of having a bitch in season in the house at least six weeks out of the year and having to maintain vigilance against the appearance of suitors during that time should be enough to discourage the practice of keeping an unspayed female. When you add to that the health benefits of early spaying, the decision should be easy.

Spayed bitches have a lower incidence of mammary tumors, a common problem in old, unspayed Beagles, and aren't likely to develop infections of the reproductive or urinary tract. If you think you really must have another Beagle just like the one you want to breed, just go back to the breeder she came from and get one. You won't have a whole litter to contend with (most people who breed one time say "never again"), and you won't be contributing to the overpopulation problem. The current belief is that female puppies should be spayed before their first heat (under six months); your vet can give the best advice here.

Altering the dog is another matter, and I am sure there have been psychological studies on why some men refuse to have their male pets altered. There is probably some parallel between this and the fact that more birth control devices and procedures have been available for women than for men. But that is another matter.

Neutering your male Beagle is inexpensive, has few, if any, complications, and will tend to make him and you better citizens. In the latter instance this is only as it applies to the overpopulation problem, as there is nothing magical about the removal of the testicles in modifying your pet's behavior. The timing of the procedure is slightly different than with spaying, since you want the dog to be sexually mature before undertaking the procedure. Otherwise he will not develop the secondary sex characteristics that identify him as a member of his gender and may appear feminine or unisex. This means waiting until he is about a year old, or whenever your vet recommends.

Neither sex will get fat just because they have been neutered. They will get fat, however, if you feed them more calories than they expend. It is as simple as that.

ADVANTAGES OF SPAY/NEUTER

The greatest advantage of spaying (for females) or neutering (for males) your dog is that you are guaranteed your dog will not produce puppies. There are too many puppies already available for too few homes. There are other advantages as well.

ADVANTAGES OF SPAYING

No messy heats.

No "suitors" howling at your windows or waiting in your yard.

Decreased incidences of pyometra (disease of the uterus) and breast cancer.

ADVANTAGES OF NEUTERING

Lessens male aggressive and territorial behaviors, but doesn't affect the dog's personality. Behaviors are often owner-induced, so neutering is not the only answer, but it is a good start.

Prevents the need to roam in search of bitches in season.

Decreased incidences of urogenital diseases.

Euthanasia

No one likes to think about the last chapters of their pet's life, but the fact is that pets don't live as long as we do. It is another fact that, like people, they are likely to have most of their medical problems, with their concomitant expense, toward the very end of their lives.

Occasionally an old hound will quietly slip away in her sleep, but more often the end is presaged by increasing infirmity and medical crises, and the old Beagle bears little resemblance to her former self. All through your pet's life, you have done everything possible to extend her life expectancy, and now the issue becomes one of quality of life.

I have seen people prolong the life of deaf, blind or incontinent hounds far beyond the realm of mere human kindness. It is hard to say good-bye to a beloved pet, a friend and member of the family, but I would encourage you, when the time comes, to consider it an act of kindness to have your pet euthanized.

Your Beagle will live to a ripe old age if you take proper care of her throughout her life.

Vets have been trained to be sensitive to the pet and the owner in these situations, and the procedure is a painless and peaceful one. Far better this than a constant battle against the inevitable deterioration that comes with advanced age and the metamorphosis of a vital animal into one you don't recognize.

You may want more information on keeping your Beagle healthy, and several excellent sources are listed in Chapter 12. On the other hand, with a little luck and a lot of Tender Loving Care, you may not ever have to refer back to this cursory review of Beagle health.

Your Happy, Healthy Pet

Your Dog's Name _____

Name on Your Dog's Pedigree (if your dog has one) _____

_____

Where Your Dog Came From _____

_____

Your Dog's Birthday _____

Your Dog's Veterinarian

    Name _____

    Address _____

    Phone Number_____

    Emergency Number_____

Your Dog's Health

    Vaccines

    type _____ date given _____

    type _____ date given _____

    type _____ date given _____

    type _____ date given _____

    Heartworm

    date tested _____ type used_____ start date _____

Your Dog's License Number_____

Groomer's Name and Number _____

Dogsitter/Walker's Name and Number_____

Awards Your Dog Has Won

    Award _____ date earned _____

    Award _____ date earned _____

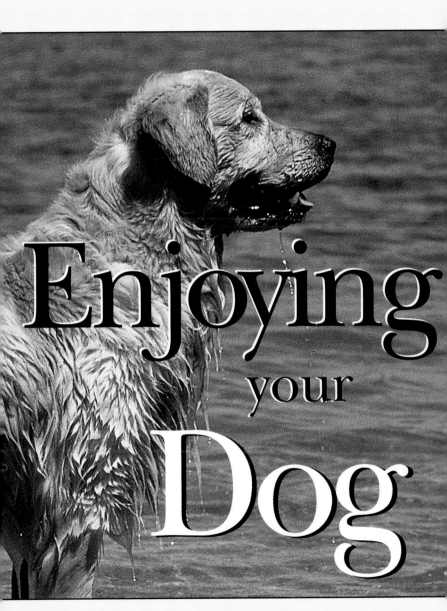

part three

Enjoying
your
Dog

chapter 8

Basic
Training

by Ian Dunbar, Ph.D., MRCVS

Training is the jewel in the crown—the most important aspect of doggy husbandry. There is no more important variable influencing dog behavior and temperament than the dog's education: A well-trained, well-behaved and good-natured puppydog is always a joy to live with, but an untrained and uncivilized dog can be a perpetual nightmare. Moreover, deny the dog an education and she will not have the opportunity to fulfill her own canine potential; neither will she have the ability to communicate effectively with her human companions.

Luckily, modern psychological training methods are easy, efficient, effective and, above all, considerably dog-friendly and user-friendly.

Doggy education is as simple as it is enjoyable. But before you can have a good time play-training with your new dog, you have to learn what to do and how to do it. There is no bigger variable influencing the success of dog training than the *owner's* experience and expertise. *Before you embark on the dog's education, you must first educate yourself.*

Basic Training for Owners

Ideally, basic owner training should begin well *before* you select your dog. Find out all you can about your chosen breed first, then master rudimentary training and handling skills. If you already have your puppy-dog, owner training is a dire emergency—the clock is ticking! Especially for puppies, the first few weeks at home are the most important and influential days in the dog's life. Indeed, the cause of most adolescent and adult problems may be traced back to the initial days the pup explores her new home. This is the time to establish the *status quo*—to teach the puppydog how you would like her to behave and so prevent otherwise quite predictable problems.

In addition to consulting breeders and breed books such as this one (which understandably have a positive breed bias), seek out as many pet owners with your breed as you can find. Good points are obvious. What you want to find out are the breed-specific *problems,* so you can nip them in the bud. In particular, you should talk to owners with *adolescent* dogs and make a list of all anticipated problems. Most important, *test drive* at least half a dozen adolescent and adult dogs of your breed yourself. An 8-week-old puppy is deceptively easy to handle, but she will acquire adult size, speed and strength in just four months, so you should learn now what to prepare for.

Puppy and pet dog training classes offer a convenient venue to locate pet owners and observe dogs in action. For a list of suitable trainers in your area, contact the Association of Pet Dog Trainers (see chapter 13). You may also begin your basic owner training by observing other owners in class. Watch as many classes and test drive as many dogs as possible. Select an upbeat, dog-friendly, people-friendly, fun-and-games, puppydog pet training class to learn the ropes. Also, watch training videos and read training books. You must find out what to do and how to do it *before* you have to do it.

Principles of Training

Most people think training comprises teaching the dog to do things such as sit, speak and roll over, but even a 4-week-old pup knows how to do these things already. Instead, the first step in training involves teaching the dog human words for each dog behavior and activity and for each aspect of the dog's environment. That way you, the owner, can more easily participate in the dog's domestic education by directing her to perform specific actions appropriately, that is, at the right time, in the right place and so on. Training opens communication channels, enabling an educated dog to at least understand her owner's requests.

In addition to teaching a dog *what* we want her to do, it is also necessary to teach her *why* she should do what we ask. Indeed, 95 percent of training revolves around motivating the dog *to want to do* what we want. Dogs often understand what their owners want; they just don't see the point of doing it—especially when the owner's repetitively boring and seemingly senseless instructions are totally at odds with much more pressing and exciting doggy distractions. It is not so much the dog that is being stubborn or dominant; rather, it is the owner who has failed to acknowledge the dog's needs and feelings and to approach training from the dog's point of view.

THE MEANING OF INSTRUCTIONS

The secret to successful training is learning how to use training lures to predict or prompt specific behaviors—to coax the dog to do what you want *when* you want. Any highly valued object (such as a treat or toy) may be used as a lure, which the dog will follow with her eyes and nose. Moving the lure in specific ways entices the dog to move her nose, head and entire body in specific ways. In fact, by learning the art of manipulating various lures, it is possible to teach the dog to assume virtually any body position and perform any action. Once you have control over the expression of the dog's behaviors and can elicit any body position or behavior at will, you can easily teach the dog to perform on request.

Teach your dog words for each activity she needs to know, like down.

Tell your dog what you want her to do, use a lure to entice her to respond correctly, then profusely praise and maybe reward her once she performs the desired action. For example, verbally request "Tina, sit!" while you move a squeaky toy upwards and backwards over the dog's muzzle (lure-movement and hand signal), smile knowingly as she looks up (to follow the lure) and sits down (as a result of canine anatomical engineering), then praise her to distraction ("Gooood Tina!"). Squeak the toy, offer a training treat and give your dog and yourself a pat on the back.

Being able to elicit desired responses over and over enables the owner to reward the dog over and over. Consequently, the dog begins to think training is fun. For example, the more the dog is rewarded for sitting, the more she enjoys sitting. Eventually the dog comes to realize that, whereas most sitting is appreciated, sitting immediately upon request usually prompts especially enthusiastic praise and a slew of high-level rewards. The dog begins to sit on cue much of the time, showing that she is starting to grasp the meaning of the owner's verbal request and hand signal.

WHY COMPLY?

Most dogs enjoy initial lure-reward training and are only too happy to comply with their owners' wishes. Unfortunately, repetitive drilling without appreciative feedback tends to diminish the dog's enthusiasm until she eventually fails to see the point of complying anymore. Moreover, as the dog approaches adolescence she becomes more easily distracted as she develops other interests. Lengthy sessions with repetitive exercises tend to bore and demotivate both parties. If it's not fun, the owner doesn't do it and neither does the dog.

Integrate training into your dog's life: The greater number of training sessions each day and the *shorter* they are, the more willingly compliant your dog will

become. Make sure to have a short (just a few seconds) training interlude before every enjoyable canine activity. For example, ask your dog to sit to greet people, to sit before you throw her Frisbee and to sit for her supper. Really, sitting is no different from a canine "Please."

To train your dog, you need gentle hands, a loving heart and a good attitude.

Also, include numerous short training interludes during every enjoyable canine pastime, for example, when playing with the dog or when she is running in the park. In this fashion, doggy distractions may be effectively converted into rewards for training. Just as all games have rules, fun becomes training . . . and training becomes fun.

Eventually, rewards actually become unnecessary to continue motivating your dog. If trained with consideration and kindness, performing the desired behaviors will become self-rewarding and, in a sense, your dog will motivate herself. Just as it is not necessary to reward a human companion during an enjoyable walk in the park, or following a game of tennis, it is hardly necessary to reward our best friend—the dog— for walking by our side or while playing fetch. Human company during enjoyable activities is reward enough for most dogs.

Even though your dog has become self-motivating, it's still good to praise and pet her a lot and offer rewards once in a while, especially for a good job well done. And if for no other reason, praising and rewarding others is good for the human heart.

PUNISHMENT

Without a doubt, lure-reward training is by far the best way to teach: Entice your dog to do what you want and then reward her for doing so. Unfortunately, a human shortcoming is to take the good for granted and to moan and groan at the bad. Specifically, the dog's many good behaviors are ignored while the owner focuses on punishing the dog for making mistakes. In extreme cases, instruction is *limited* to punishing mistakes made by a trainee dog, child, employee or husband, even though it has been proven punishment training is notoriously inefficient and ineffective and is decidedly unfriendly and combative. It teaches the dog that training is a drag, almost as quickly as it teaches the dog to dislike her trainer. Why treat our best friends like our worst enemies?

Punishment training is also much more laborious and time consuming. Whereas it takes only a finite amount of time to teach a dog what to chew, for example, it takes much, much longer to punish the dog for each and every mistake. Remember, *there is only one right way!* So why not teach that right way from the outset?!

To make matters worse, punishment training causes severe lapses in the dog's reliability. Since it is obviously impossible to punish the dog each and every time she misbehaves, the dog quickly learns to distinguish between those times when she must comply (so as to avoid impending punishment) and those times when she need not comply, because punishment is impossible. Such times include when the dog is off leash and 6 feet away, when the owner is otherwise engaged (talking to a friend, watching television, taking a shower, tending to the baby or chatting on the telephone) or when the dog is left at home alone.

Instances of misbehavior will be numerous when the owner is away, because even when the dog complied in the owner's looming presence, she did so unwillingly. The dog was forced to act against her will, rather than molding her will to want to please. Hence, when the owner is absent, not only does the dog know she need not comply, she simply does not want to. Again, the trainee is not a stubborn vindictive beast, but rather the trainer has failed to teach. Punishment training invariably creates unpredictable Jekyll and Hyde behavior.

Trainer's Tools

Many training books extol the virtues of a vast array of training paraphernalia and electronic and metallic gizmos, most of which are designed for canine restraint, correction and punishment, rather than for actual facilitation of doggy education. In reality, most effective training tools are not found in stores; they come from within ourselves. In addition to a willing dog, all you really need is a functional human brain, gentle hands, a loving heart and a good attitude.

In terms of equipment, all dogs do require a quality buckle collar to sport dog tags and to attach the leash (for safety and to comply with local leash laws). Hollow chew toys (like Kongs or sterilized longbones) and a dog bed or collapsible crate are musts for housetraining. Three additional tools are required:

1. specific lures (training treats and toys) to predict and prompt specific desired behaviors;
2. rewards (praise, affection, training treats and toys) to reinforce for the dog what a lot of fun it all is; and
3. knowledge—how to convert the dog's favorite activities and games (potential distractions to training) into "life-rewards," which may be employed to facilitate training.

The most powerful of these is *knowledge*. Education is the key! Watch training classes, participate in training classes, watch videos, read books, enjoy play-training with your dog and then your dog will say "Please," and your dog will say "Thank you!"

Housetraining

If dogs were left to their own devices, certainly they would chew, dig and bark for entertainment and then no doubt highlight a few areas of their living space with sprinkles of urine, in much the same way we decorate by hanging pictures. Consequently, when we ask a dog to live with us, we must teach her *where* she may dig, *where* she may perform her toilet duties, *what* she may chew and *when* she may bark. After all, when left at home alone for many hours, we cannot expect the dog to amuse herself by completing crosswords or watching the soaps on TV!

Also, it would be decidedly unfair to keep the house rules a secret from the dog, and then get angry and punish the poor critter for inevitably transgressing rules she did not even know existed. Remember: Without adequate education and guidance, the dog will be forced to establish her own rules—doggy rules—and most probably will be at odds with the owner's view of domestic living.

Since most problems develop during the first few days the dog is at home, prospective dog owners must be certain they are quite clear about the principles of housetraining *before* they get a dog. Early misbehaviors quickly become established as the *status quo*—

becoming firmly entrenched as hard-to-break bad
habits, which set the precedent for years to come.
Make sure to teach your dog good habits right from
the start. Good habits are just as hard to break as bad
ones!

Ideally, when a new dog comes home, try to arrange
for someone to be present as much as possible during
the first few days (for adult dogs) or weeks for puppies.
With only a little forethought, it is surprisingly easy to
find a puppy sitter, such as a retired person, who would
be willing to eat from your refrigerator and watch your
television while keeping an eye on the newcomer to
encourage the dog to play with chew toys and to ensure
she goes outside on a regular basis.

POTTY TRAINING

To teach the dog where to relieve herself:

1. never let her make a single mistake;
2. let her know where you want her to go; and
3. handsomely reward her for doing so:
   "GOOOOOOOD DOG!!!" liver treat, liver treat,
   liver treat!

Preventing Mistakes

A single mistake is a training disaster, since it heralds
many more in future weeks. And each time the dog
soils the house, this further reinforces the dog's unfortunate preference for an indoor, carpeted toilet.
*Do not let an unhousetrained dog have full run of the
house.*

When you are away from home, or cannot pay full attention, confine the dog to an area where elimination is
appropriate, such as an outdoor run or, better still, a
small, comfortable indoor kennel with access to an outdoor run. When confined in this manner, most dogs
will naturally housetrain themselves.

If that's not possible, confine the dog to an area, such
as a utility room, kitchen, basement or garage, where

elimination may not be desired in the long run but as an interim measure it is certainly preferable to doing it all around the house. Use newspaper to cover the floor of the dog's day room. The newspaper may be used to soak up the urine and to wrap up and dispose of the feces. Once your dog develops a preferred spot for eliminating, it is only necessary to cover that part of the floor with newspaper. The smaller papered area may then be moved (only a little each day) towards the door to the outside. Thus the dog will develop the tendency to go to the door when she needs to relieve herself.

Never confine an unhousetrained dog to a crate for long periods. Doing so would force the dog to soil the crate and ruin its usefulness as an aid for housetraining (see the following discussion).

Teaching Where

In order to teach your dog where you would like her to do her business, you have to be there to direct the proceedings—an obvious, yet often neglected, fact of life. In order to be there to teach the dog *where* to go, you need to know *when* she needs to go. Indeed, the success of housetraining depends on the owner's ability to predict these times. Certainly, a regular feeding schedule will facilitate prediction somewhat, but there is nothing like "loading the deck" and influencing the timing of the outcome yourself!

The first few weeks at home are the most important and influential in your dog's life.

Whenever you are at home, make sure the dog is under constant supervision and/or confined to a small area. If already well trained, simply instruct the dog to lie down in her bed or basket. Alternatively, confine the dog to a crate (doggy den) or tie-down (a short, 18-inch lead that can be clipped to an eye hook in the baseboard near her bed). Short-term close confinement strongly inhibits urination and defecation, since the dog does not want to soil her sleeping area. Thus, when you release the puppydog each hour, she will definitely need to urinate immediately and defecate every third or fourth hour. Keep the dog confined to her doggy den and take her to her intended toilet area each hour, every hour and on the hour.

When taking your dog outside, instruct her to sit quietly before opening the door—she will soon learn to sit by the door when she needs to go out!

Teaching Why

Being able to predict when the dog needs to go enables the owner to be on the spot to praise and reward the dog. Each hour, hurry the dog to the intended toilet area in the yard, issue the appropriate instruction ("Go pee!" or "Go poop!"), then give the dog three to four minutes to produce. Praise and offer a couple of training treats when successful. The treats are important because many people fail to praise their dogs with feeling . . . and housetraining is hardly the time for understatement. So either loosen up and enthusiastically praise that dog: "Wuzzzer-wuzzer-wuzzer, hoooser good wuffer den? Hoooo went pee for Daddy?" Or say "Good dog!" as best you can and offer the treats for effect.

Following elimination is an ideal time for a spot of play-training in the yard or house. Also, an empty dog may be allowed greater freedom around the house for the next half hour or so, just as long as you keep an eye out to make sure she does not get into other kinds of mischief. If you are preoccupied and cannot pay full attention, confine the dog to her doggy den once more to enjoy a peaceful snooze or to play with her many chew toys.

If your dog does not eliminate within the allotted time outside—no biggie! Back to her doggy den, and then try again after another hour.

As I own large dogs, I always feel more relaxed walking an empty dog, knowing that I will not need to finish our stroll weighted down with bags of feces!

Beware of falling into the trap of walking the dog to get her to eliminate. The good ol' dog walk is such an enormous highlight in the dog's life that it represents the single biggest potential reward in domestic dogdom. However, when in a hurry, or during inclement weather, many owners abruptly terminate the walk the moment the dog has done her business. This, in effect, severely punishes the dog for doing the right thing, in the right place at the right time. Consequently, many dogs become strongly inhibited from eliminating outdoors because they know it will signal an abrupt end to an otherwise thoroughly enjoyable walk.

Instead, instruct the dog to relieve herself in the yard prior to going for a walk. If you follow the above instructions, most dogs soon learn to eliminate on cue. As soon as the dog eliminates, praise (and offer a treat or two)—"Good dog! Let's go walkies!" Use the walk as a reward for eliminating in the yard. If the dog does not go, put her back in her doggy den and think about a walk later on. You will find with a "No feces—no walk" policy, your dog will become one of the fastest defecators in the business.

If you do not have a backyard, instruct the dog to eliminate right outside your front door prior to the walk. Not only will this facilitate clean up and disposal of the feces in your own trash can but, also, the walk may again be used as a colossal reward.

CHEWING AND BARKING

Short-term close confinement also teaches the dog that occasional quiet moments are a reality of domestic living. Your puppydog is extremely impressionable during her first few weeks at home. Regular

109

confinement at this time soon exerts a calming influence over the dog's personality. Remember, once the dog is housetrained and calmer, there will be a whole lifetime ahead for the dog to enjoy full run of the house and garden. On the other hand, by letting the newcomer have unrestricted access to the entire household and allowing her to run willy-nilly, she will most certainly develop a bunch of behavior problems in short order, no doubt necessitating confinement later in life. It would not be fair to remedially restrain and confine a dog you have trained, through neglect, to run free.

When confining the dog, make sure she always has an impressive array of suitable chew toys. Kongs and sterilized longbones (both readily available from pet stores) make the best chew toys, since they are hollow and may be stuffed with treats to heighten the dog's interest. For example, by stuffing the little hole at the top of a Kong with a small piece of freeze-dried liver, the dog will not want to leave it alone.

Remember, treats do not have to be junk food and they certainly should not represent extra calories. Rather, treats should be part of each dog's regular

daily diet: Some food may be served in the dog's bowl for breakfast and dinner, some food may be used as training treats, and some food may be used for stuffing chew toys. I regularly stuff my dogs' many Kongs with different shaped biscuits and kibble.

Make sure your puppy has suitable chew toys.

The kibble seems to fall out fairly easily, as do the oval-shaped biscuits, thus rewarding the dog instantaneously for checking out the chew toys. The bone-shaped biscuits fall out after a while, rewarding the dog for worrying at the chew toy. But the triangular biscuits never come out. They remain inside the Kong as lures, maintaining the dog's fascination with her chew toy. To further focus the dog's interest, I always make sure to flavor the triangular biscuits by rubbing them with a little cheese or freeze-dried liver.

To teach come, call your dog, open your arms as a welcoming signal, wave a toy or a treat and praise for every step in your direction.

If stuffed chew toys are reserved especially for times the dog is confined, the puppydog will soon learn to enjoy quiet moments in her doggy den and she will quickly develop a chew-toy habit— a good habit! This is a simple *autoshaping* process; all the owner has to do is set up the situation and the dog all but trains herself— easy and effective. Even when the dog is given run of the house, her first inclination will be to indulge her rewarding chew-toy habit rather than destroy less-attractive household articles, such as curtains, carpets, chairs and compact disks. Similarly, a chew-toy chewer will be less inclined to scratch and chew herself excessively. Also, if the dog busies herself as a recreational chewer, she will be less inclined to develop into a recreational barker or digger when left at home alone.

Stuff a number of chew toys whenever the dog is left confined and remove the extra-special-tasting treats when you return. Your dog will now amuse herself with her chew toys before falling asleep and then resume playing with her chew toys when she expects you to return. Since most owner-absent misbehavior happens right after you leave and right before your expected return, your puppydog will now be conveniently preoccupied with her chew toys at these times.

Come and Sit

Most puppies will happily approach virtually anyone, whether called or not; that is, until they collide with adolescence and develop other more important doggy interests, such as sniffing a multiplicity of exquisite odors on the grass. Your mission, Mr./Ms. Owner, is to teach and reward the pup for coming reliably, willingly and happily when called—and you have just three months to get it done. Unless adequately reinforced, your puppy's tendency to approach people will self-destruct by adolescence.

Call your dog ("Tina, come!"), open your arms (and maybe squat down) as a welcoming signal, waggle a treat or toy as a lure and reward the puppydog when she comes running. Do not wait to praise the dog until she reaches you—she may come 95 percent of the way and then run off after some distraction. Instead, praise the dog's *first* step towards you and continue praising enthusiastically for *every* step she takes in your direction.

When the rapidly approaching puppy dog is three lengths away from impact, instruct her to sit ("Tina, sit!") and hold the lure in front of you in an outstretched hand to prevent her from hitting you midchest and knocking you flat on your back! As Tina decelerates to nose the lure, move the treat upwards and backwards just over her muzzle with an upwards motion of your extended arm (palm-upwards). As the dog looks up to follow the lure, she will sit down (if she jumps up, you are holding the lure too high). Praise the dog for sitting. Move backwards and call her again. Repeat this many times over, always praising when Tina comes and sits; on occasion, reward her.

For the first couple of trials, use a training treat both as a lure to entice the dog to come and sit and as a reward for doing so. Thereafter, try to use different items as lures and rewards. For example, lure the dog with a Kong or Frisbee but reward her with a food treat. Or lure the dog with a food treat but pat her and throw a tennis ball as a reward. After just a few repetitions, dispense with the lures and rewards; the dog will begin to respond willingly to your verbal requests and hand signals just for the prospect of praise from your heart and affection from your hands.

Instruct every family member, friend and visitor how to get the dog to come and sit. Invite people over for a series of pooch parties; do not keep the pup a secret— let other people enjoy this puppy, and let the pup enjoy other people. Puppydog parties are not only fun, they easily attract a lot of people to help *you* train *your* dog. Unless you teach your dog how to meet people, that is, to sit for greetings, no doubt the dog will resort to jumping up. Then you and the visitors will get annoyed, and the dog will be punished. This is not fair. *Send out those invitations for puppy parties and teach your dog to be mannerly and socially acceptable.*

Even though your dog quickly masters obedient recalls in the house, her reliability may falter when playing in the backyard or local park. Ironically, it is *the owner* who has unintentionally trained the dog *not* to respond in these instances. By allowing the dog to play and run around and otherwise have a good time, but then to call the dog to put her on leash to take her home, the dog quickly learns playing is fun but training is a drag. Thus, playing in the park becomes a severe distraction, which works against training. Bad news!

Instead, whether playing with the dog off leash or on leash, request her to come at frequent intervals—say, every minute or so. On most occasions, praise and pet the dog for a few seconds while she is sitting, then tell her to go play again. For especially fast recalls, offer a couple of training treats and take the time to praise and pet the dog enthusiastically before releasing her. The dog will learn that coming when called is not necessarily the end of the play session, and neither is it the end of the world; rather, it signals an enjoyable, quality time-out with the owner before resuming play once more. In fact, playing in the park now becomes a very effective life-reward, which works to facilitate training by reinforcing each obedient and timely recall. Good news!

Sit, Down, Stand and Rollover
Teaching the dog a variety of body positions is easy for owner and dog, impressive for spectators and

113

extremely useful for all. Using lure-reward techniques, it is possible to train several positions at once to verbal commands or hand signals (which impress the socks off onlookers).

Sit and ***down***—the two control commands—prevent or resolve nearly a hundred behavior problems. For example, if the dog happily and obediently sits or lies down when requested, she cannot jump on visitors, dash out the front door, run around and chase her tail, pester other dogs, harass cats or annoy family, friends or strangers. Additionally, "Sit" or "Down" are the best emergency commands for off-leash control.

It is easier to teach and maintain a reliable sit than maintain a reliable recall. *Sit* is the purest and simplest of commands—either the dog is sitting or she is not. If there is any change of circumstances or potential danger in the park, for example, simply instruct the dog to sit. If she sits, you have a number of options: Allow the dog to resume playing when she is safe, walk up and put the dog on leash or call the dog. The dog will be much more likely to come when called if she has already acknowledged her compliance by sitting. If the dog does not sit in the park—train her to!

Stand and *rollover-stay* are the two positions for examining the dog. Your veterinarian will love you to distraction if you take a little time to teach the dog to stand still and roll over and play possum. Also, your vet bills will be smaller because it will take the veterinarian less time to examine your dog. The rollover-stay is an especially useful command and is really just a variation of the down-stay: Whereas the dog lies prone in the traditional down, she lies supine in the rollover-stay.

As with teaching come and sit, the training techniques to teach the dog to assume all other body positions on cue are user-friendly and dog-friendly. Simply give the appropriate request, lure the dog into the desired body position using a training treat or toy and then *praise* (and maybe reward) the dog as soon as she complies. Try not to touch the dog to get her to respond. If you teach the dog by guiding her into position, the dog will quickly learn that rump-pressure means sit, for example, but as yet you still have no control over your dog if she is just 6 feet away. It will still be necessary to teach the dog to sit on request. So do not make training a time-consuming two-step process; instead, teach the dog to sit to a verbal request or hand signal from the outset. Once the dog sits willingly when requested, by all means use your hands to pet the dog when she does so.

To teach *down* when the dog is already sitting, say "Tina, down!," hold the lure in one hand (palm down) and lower that hand to the floor between the dog's forepaws. As the dog lowers her head to follow the lure, slowly move the lure away from the dog just a fraction (in front of her paws). The dog will lie down as she stretches her nose forward to follow the lure. Praise the dog when she does so. If the dog stands up, you pulled the lure away too far and too quickly.

When teaching the dog to lie down from the standing position, say "Down" and lower the lure to the floor as before. Once the dog has lowered her forequarters and assumed a play bow, gently and slowly move the lure *towards* the dog between her forelegs. Praise the dog as soon as her rear end plops down.

After just a couple of trials it will be possible to alternate sits and downs and have the dog energetically perform doggy push-ups. Praise the dog a lot, and after half a dozen or so push-ups reward the dog with a training treat or toy. You will notice the more energetically you move your arm—upwards (palm up) to get the dog to sit, and downwards (palm down) to get the dog to lie down—the more energetically the dog responds to your requests. Now try training the dog in silence and you will notice she has also learned to respond to hand signals. Yeah! Not too shabby for the first session.

To teach *stand* from the sitting position, say "Tina, stand," slowly move the lure half a dog-length away from the dog's nose, keeping it at nose level, and praise the dog as she stands to follow the lure. As soon

Using a food lure to teach sit, down and stand. 1) "Phoenix, sit." 2) Hand palm upwards, move lure up and back over dog's muzzle. 3) "Good sit, Phoenix!" 4) "Phoenix, down." 5) Hand palm downwards, move lure down to lie between dog's forepaws. 6) "Phoenix, off. Good down, Phoenix!" 7) "Phoenix, sit!" 8) Palm upwards, move lure up and back, keeping it close to dog's muzzle. 9) "Good sit, Phoenix!"

10) *"Phoenix, stand!"* 11) *Move lure away from dog at nose height, then lower it a tad.* 12) *"Phoenix, off! Good stand, Phoenix!"* 13) *"Phoenix, down!"* 14) *Hand palm downwards, move lure down to lie between dog's forepaws.* 15) *"Phoenix, off! Good down-stay, Phoenix!"* 16) *"Phoenix, stand!"* 17) *Move lure away from dog's muzzle up to nose height.* 18) *"Phoenix, off! Good stand-stay, Phoenix. Now we'll make the vet and groomer happy!"*

Enjoying Your
Dog

as the dog stands, lower the lure to just beneath the
dog's chin to entice her to look down; otherwise she
will stand and then sit immediately. To prompt the dog
to stand from the down position, move the lure half a
dog-length upwards and away from the dog, holding
the lure at standing nose height from the floor.

Teaching *rollover* is best started from the down position, with the dog lying on one side, or at least with
both hind legs stretched out on the same side. Say
"Tina, bang!" and move the lure backwards and along-
side the dog's muzzle to her elbow (on the side of her
outstretched hind legs). Once the dog looks to the side
and backwards, very slowly move the lure upwards to
the dog's shoulder and backbone. Tickling the dog in
the goolies (groin area) often invokes a reflex-raising
of the hind leg as an appeasement gesture, which facilitates the tendency to roll over. If you move the lure
too quickly and the dog jumps into the standing position, have patience and start again. As soon as the dog
rolls onto her back, keep the lure stationary and mes-
merize the dog with a relaxing tummy rub.

To teach *rollover-stay* when the dog is standing or mov-
ing, say "Tina, bang!" and give the appropriate hand
signal (with index finger pointed and thumb cocked in
true Sam Spade fashion), then in one fluid movement
lure her to first lie down and then rollover-stay as above.

Teaching the dog to *stay* in each of the above four positions becomes a piece of cake after first teaching the
dog not to worry at the toy or treat training lure. This
is best accomplished by hand feeding dinner kibble.
Hold a piece of kibble firmly in your hand and softly
instruct "Off!" Ignore any licking and slobbering *for
however long the dog worries at the treat*, but say "Take it!"
and offer the kibble *the instant* the dog breaks contact
with her muzzle. Repeat this a few times, and then up
the ante and insist the dog remove her muzzle for one
whole second before offering the kibble. Then progressively refine your criteria and have the dog
not touch your hand (or treat) for longer and longer
periods on each trial, such as for two seconds, four

seconds, then six, ten, fifteen, twenty, thirty seconds and so on.

The dog soon learns: (1) worrying at the treat never gets results, whereas (2) noncontact is often rewarded after a variable time lapse.

Teaching *"Off!"* has many useful applications in its own right. Additionally, instructing the dog not to touch a training lure often produces spontaneous and magical stays. Request the dog to stand-stay, for example, and not to touch the lure. At first set your sights on a short two-second stay before rewarding the dog. (Remember, every long journey begins with a single step.) However, on subsequent trials, gradually and progressively increase the length of stay required to receive a reward. In no time at all your dog will stand calmly for a minute or so.

Relevancy Training

Once you have taught the dog what you expect her to do when requested to come, sit, lie down, stand, roll-over and stay, the time is right to teach the dog *why* she should comply with your wishes. The secret is to have many (*many*) extremely short training interludes (two to five seconds each) at numerous (*numerous*) times during the course of the dog's day. Especially work with the dog immediately *before* the dog's good times and *during* the dog's good times. For example, ask your dog to sit and/or lie down each time before opening doors, serving meals, offering treats and tummy rubs; ask the dog to perform a few controlled doggy push-ups before letting her off leash or throwing a tennis ball; and perhaps request the dog to sit-down-sit-stand-down-stand-rollover before inviting her to cuddle on the couch.

Similarly, request the dog to sit many times during play or on walks, and in no time at all the dog will be only too pleased to follow your instructions because she has learned that a compliant response heralds all sorts of goodies. Basically all you are trying to teach the dog is how to say please: "Please throw the tennis ball. Please may I snuggle on the couch."

Remember, it is important to keep training interludes short and to have many short sessions each and every day. The shortest (and most useful) session comprises asking the dog to sit and then go play during a play session. When trained this way, your dog will soon associate training with good times. In fact, the dog may be unable to distinguish between training and good times and, indeed, there should be no distinction. The warped concept that training involves forcing the dog to comply and/or dominating her will is totally at odds with the picture of a truly well-trained dog. In reality, enjoying a game of training with a dog is no different from enjoying a game of backgammon or tennis with a friend; and walking with a dog should be no different from strolling with a spouse, or with buddies on the golf course.

Walk by Your Side

Many people attempt to teach a dog to heel by putting her on a leash and physically correcting the dog when she makes mistakes. There are a number of things seriously wrong with this approach, the first being that most people do not want precision heeling; rather, they simply want the dog to follow or walk by their side. Second, when physically restrained during "training," even though the dog may grudgingly mope by your side when "handcuffed" on leash, let's see what happens when she is off leash. History! The dog is in the next county because she never enjoyed walking with you on leash and you have no control over her off leash. So let's just teach the dog off leash from the outset to *want* to walk with us. Third, if the dog has not been trained to heel, it is a trifle hasty to think about punishing the poor dog for making mistakes and breaking heeling rules she didn't even know existed. This is simply not fair! Surely, if the dog had been adequately taught how to heel, she would seldom make mistakes and hence there would be no need to correct the dog. Remember, each mistake and each correction (punishment) advertise the trainer's inadequacy, not the dog's. The dog is not stubborn, she is not stupid and she is not bad. Even if she were, she would still require training, so let's train her properly.

Let's teach the dog to *enjoy* following us and to *want* to walk by our side off leash. Then it will be easier to teach high-precision off-leash heeling patterns if desired. Before going on outdoor walks, it is necessary to teach the dog not to pull. Then it becomes easy to teach on-leash walking and heeling because the dog already wants to walk with you, she is familiar with the desired walking and heeling positions and she knows not to pull.

FOLLOWING

Start by training your dog to follow you. Many puppies will follow if you simply walk away from them and maybe click your fingers or chuckle. Adult dogs may require additional enticement to stimulate them to follow, such as a training lure or, at the very least, a lively trainer. To teach the dog to follow: (1) keep walking and (2) walk away from the dog. If the dog attempts to lead or lag, change pace; slow down if the dog forges too far ahead, but speed up if she lags too far behind. Say "Steady!" or "Easy!" each time before you slow down and "Quickly!" or "Hustle!" each time before you speed up, and the dog will learn to change pace on cue. If the dog lags or leads too far, or if she wanders right or left, simply walk quickly in the opposite direction and maybe even run away from the dog and hide.

Practicing is a lot of fun; you can set up a course in your home, yard or park to do this. Indoors, entice the dog to follow upstairs, into a bedroom, into the bathroom, downstairs, around the living room couch, zigzagging between dining room chairs and into the kitchen for dinner. Outdoors, get the dog to follow around park benches, trees, shrubs and along walkways and lines in the grass. (For safety outdoors, it is advisable to attach a long line on the dog, but never exert corrective tension on the line.)

121

Remember, following has a lot to do with attitude—*your* attitude! Most probably your dog will *not* want to follow Mr. Grumpy Troll with the personality of wilted lettuce. Lighten up—walk with a jaunty step, whistle a happy tune, sing, skip and tell jokes to your dog and she will be right there by your side.

BY YOUR SIDE

It is smart to train the dog to walk close on one side or the other—either side will do, your choice. When walking, jogging or cycling, it is generally bad news to have the dog suddenly cut in front of you. In fact, I train my dogs to walk "By my side" and "Other side"—both very useful instructions. It is possible to position the dog fairly accurately by looking to the appropriate side and clicking your fingers or slapping your thigh on that side. A precise positioning may be attained by holding a training lure, such as a chew toy, tennis ball or food treat. Stop and stand still several times throughout the walk, just as you would when window shopping or meeting a friend. Use the lure to make sure the dog slows down and stays close whenever you stop.

When teaching the dog to heel, we generally want her to sit in heel position when we stop. Teach heel

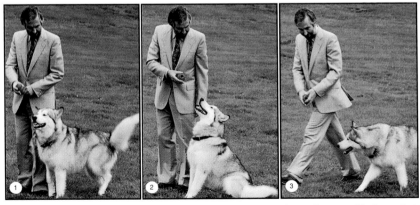

Using a toy to teach sit-heel-sit sequences: 1) "Phoenix, sit!" Standing still, move lure up and back over dog's muzzle . . . 2) to position dog sitting in heel position on your left side. 3) Say "Phoenix, heel!" and walk ahead, wagging lure in left hand. Change lure to right hand in preparation for sit signal. Say "Sit" and then . . .

position at the standstill and the dog will learn that the default heel position is sitting by your side (left or right—your choice, unless you wish to compete in obedience trials, in which case the dog must heel on the left).

Several times a day, stand up and call your dog to come and sit in heel position—"Tina, heel!" For example, instruct the dog to come to heel each time there are commercials on TV, or each time you turn a page of a novel, and the dog will get it in a single evening.

Practice straight-line heeling and turns separately. With the dog sitting at heel, teach her to turn in place. After each quarter-turn, half-turn or full turn in place, lure the dog to sit at heel. Now it's time for short straight-line heeling sequences, no more than a few steps at a time. Always think of heeling in terms of sit-heel-sit sequences—start and end with the dog in position and do your best to keep her there when moving. Progressively increase the number of steps in each sequence. When the dog remains close for 20 yards of straight-line heeling, it is time to add a few turns and then sign up for a happy-heeling obedience class to get some advice from the experts.

4) use hand signal to lure dog to sit as you stop. Eventually, dog will sit automatically at heel whenever you stop. 5) "Good dog!"

No Pulling on Leash

You can start teaching your dog not to pull on leash
anywhere—in front of the television or outdoors—but
regardless of location, you must not take a single step
with tension in the leash. For a reason known only to
dogs, even just a couple of paces of pulling on leash is
intrinsically motivating and diabolically rewarding.
Instead, attach the leash to the dog's collar, grasp the
other end firmly with both hands held close to your
chest, and stand still—do not budge an inch. Have
somebody watch you with a stopwatch to time your
progress, or else you will never believe this will work
and so you will not even try the exercise, and your
shoulder and the dog's neck will be traumatized for
years to come.

Stand still and wait for the dog to stop pulling, and to
sit and/or lie down. All dogs stop pulling and sit eventually. Most take only a couple of minutes; the all-time
record is $22\frac{1}{2}$ minutes. Time how long it takes. Gently
praise the dog when she stops pulling, and as soon as
she sits, enthusiastically praise the dog and take just one
step forward, then immediately stand still. This single
step usually demonstrates the ballistic reinforcing
nature of pulling on leash; most dogs explode to the
end of the leash, so be prepared for the strain. Stand
firm and wait for the dog to sit again. Repeat this half a
dozen times and you will probably notice a progressive
reduction in the force of the dog's one-step explosions
and a radical reduction in the time it takes for the dog
to sit each time.

As the dog learns "Sit we go" and "Pull we stop," she
will begin to walk forward calmly with each single step
and automatically sit when you stop. Now try two steps
before you stop. Wooooooo! Scary! When the dog has
mastered two steps at a time, try for three. After each
success, progressively increase the number of steps in
the sequence: try four steps and then six, eight, ten
and twenty steps before stopping. Congratulations! You
are now walking the dog on leash.

Whenever walking with the dog (off leash or on leash), make sure you stop periodically to practice a few position commands and stays before instructing the dog to "Walk on!" (Remember, you want the dog to be compliant everywhere, not just in the kitchen when her dinner is at hand.) For example, stopping every 25 yards to briefly train the dog amounts to over 200 training interludes within a single 3-mile stroll. And each training session is in a different location. You will not believe the improvement within just the first mile of the first walk.

To put it another way, integrating training into a walk offers 200 separate opportunities to use the continuance of the walk as a reward to reinforce the dog's education. Moreover, some training interludes may comprise continuing education for the dog's walking skills: Alternate short periods of the dog walking calmly by your side with periods when the dog is allowed to sniff and investigate the environment. Now sniffing odors on the grass and meeting other dogs become rewards which reinforce the dog's calm and mannerly demeanor. Good Lord! Whatever next? Many enjoyable walks together of course. Happy trails!

Enjoying
Your
Dog

THE IMPORTANCE OF TRICKS

Nothing will improve a dog's quality of life better than having a few tricks under her belt. Teaching any trick expands the dog's vocabulary, which facilitates communication and improves the owner's control. Also, specific tricks help prevent and resolve specific behavior problems. For example, by teaching the dog to fetch her toys, the dog learns carrying a toy makes the owner happy and, therefore, will be more likely to chew her toy than other inappropriate items.

More important, teaching tricks prompts owners to lighten up and train with a sunny disposition. Really, tricks should be no different from any other behaviors we put on cue. But they are. When teaching tricks, owners have a much sweeter attitude, which in turn motivates the dog and improves her willingness to comply. The dog feels tricks are a blast, but formal commands are a drag. In fact, tricks are so enjoyable, they may be used as rewards in training by asking the dog to come, sit and down-stay and then rollover for a tummy rub. Go on, try it: Crack a smile and even giggle when the dog promptly and willingly lies down and stays.

Most important, performing tricks prompts onlookers to smile and giggle. Many people are scared of dogs, especially large ones. And nothing can be more off-putting for a dog than to be constantly confronted by strangers who don't like her because of her size or the way she looks. Uneasy people put the dog on edge, causing her to back off and bark, only frightening people all the more. And so a vicious circle develops, with the people's fear fueling the dog's fear *and vice versa*. Instead, tie a pink ribbon to your dog's collar and practice all sorts of tricks on walks and in the park, and you will be pleasantly amazed how it changes people's attitudes toward your friendly dog. The dog's repertoire of tricks is limited only by the trainer's imagination. Below I have described three of my favorites:

SPEAK AND SHUSH

The training sequence involved in teaching a dog to bark on request is no different from that used when training any behavior on cue: request—lure—response—reward. As always, the secret of success lies in finding an effective lure. If the dog always barks at the doorbell, for example, say "Rover, speak!", have an accomplice ring the doorbell, then reward the dog for barking. After a few woofs, ask Rover to "Shush!", waggle a food treat under her nose (to entice her to sniff and thus to shush), praise her when quiet and eventually offer the treat as a reward. Alternate "Speak" and "Shush," progressively increasing the length of shush-time between each barking bout.

PLAY BOW

With the dog standing, say "Bow!" and lower the food lure (palm upwards) to rest between the dog's forepaws. Praise as the dog lowers

her forequarters and sternum to the ground (as when teaching the down), but then lure the dog to stand and offer the treat. On successive trials, gradually increase the length of time the dog is required to remain in the play bow posture in order to gain a food reward. If the dog's rear end collapses into a down, say nothing and offer no reward; simply start over.

BE A BEAR

With the dog sitting backed into a corner to prevent her from toppling over backwards, say "Be a bear!" With bent paw and palm down, raise a lure upwards and backwards along the top of the dog's muzzle. Praise the dog when she sits up on her haunches and offer the treat as a reward. To prevent the dog from standing on her hind legs, keep the lure closer to the dog's muzzle. On each trial, progressively increase the length of time the dog is required to sit up to receive a food reward. Since lure-reward training is so easy, teach the dog to stand and walk on her hind legs as well!

Teaching "Be a Bear"

chapter 9

Getting
Active
with your Dog

by Bardi McLennan

Once you and your dog have graduated from basic obedience training and are beginning to work together as a team, you can take part in the growing world of dog activities. There are so many fun things to do with your dog! Just remember, people and dogs don't always learn at the same pace, so don't be upset if you (or your dog) need more than two basic training courses before your team becomes operational. Even smart dogs don't go straight to college from kindergarten!

Just as there are events geared to certain types of dogs, so there are ones that are more appealing to certain types of people. In some activities, you give the commands and your dog does the work (upland game hunting is one example), while in others, such as agility, you'll both get a workout. You may want to aim for prestigious titles to add to your dog's name, or you may want nothing more than the sheer enjoyment of being around other people and their dogs. Passive or active, participation has its own rewards.

Consider your dog's physical capabilities when looking into any of the canine activities. It's easy to see that a Basset Hound is not built for the racetrack, nor would a Chihuahua be the breed of choice for pulling a sled. A loyal dog will attempt almost anything you ask him to do, so it is up to you to know your dog's limitations. A dog must be physically sound in order to compete at any level in athletic activities, and being mentally sound is a definite plus. Advanced age, however, may not be a deterrent. Many dogs still hunt and herd at ten or twelve years of age. It's entirely possible for dogs to be "fit at 50." Take your dog for a checkup, explain to your vet the type of activity you have in mind and be guided by his or her findings.

All dogs seem to love playing flyball.

You needn't be restricted to breed-specific sports if it's only fun you're after. Certain AKC activities are limited to designated breeds; however, as each new trial, test or sport has grown in popularity, so has the variety of breeds encouraged to participate at a fun level.

But don't shortchange your fun, or that of your dog, by thinking only of the basic function of her breed. Once a dog has learned how to learn, she can be taught to do just about anything as long as the size of the dog is right for the job and you both think it is fun and rewarding. In other words, you are a team.

129

To get involved in any of the activities detailed in this chapter, look for the names and addresses of the organizations that sponsor them in Chapter 13. You can also ask your breeder or a local dog trainer for contacts.

You can compete in obedience trials with a well trained dog.

Official American Kennel Club Activities

The following tests and trials are some of the events sanctioned by the AKC and sponsored by various dog clubs. Your dog's expertise will be rewarded with impressive titles. You can participate just for fun, or be competitive and go for those awards.

OBEDIENCE

Training classes begin with pups as young as three months of age in kindergarten puppy training, then advance to pre-novice (all exercises on lead) and go on to novice, which is where you'll start off-lead work. In obedience classes dogs learn to sit, stay, heel and come through a variety of exercises. Once you've got the basics down, you can enter obedience trials and work toward earning your dog's first degree, a C.D. (Companion Dog).

The next level is called "Open," in which jumps and retrieves perk up the dog's interest. Passing grades in competition at this level earn a C.D.X. (Companion Dog Excellent). Beyond that lies the goal of the most ambitious—Utility (U.D. and even U.D.X. or OTCh, an Obedience Champion).

AGILITY

All dogs can participate in the latest canine sport to have gained worldwide popularity for its fun and excitement, agility. It began in England as a canine version of horse show-jumping, but because dogs are more agile and able to perform on verbal commands, extra feats were added such as climbing, balancing and racing through tunnels or in and out of weave poles.

Many of the obstacles (regulation or homemade) can be set up in your own backyard. If the agility bug bites, you could end up in international competition!

For starters, your dog should be obedience trained, even though, in the beginning, the lessons may all be taught on lead. Once the dog understands the commands (and you do, too), it's as easy as guiding the dog over a prescribed course, one obstacle at a time. In competition, the race is against the clock, so wear your running shoes! The dog starts with 200 points and the judge deducts for infractions and misadventures along the way.

All dogs seem to love agility and respond to it as if they were being turned loose in a playground paradise. Your dog's enthusiasm will be contagious; agility turns into great fun for dog and owner.

FIELD TRIALS AND HUNTING TESTS

There are field trials and hunting tests for the sporting breeds—retrievers, spaniels and pointing breeds, and for some hounds—Bassets, Beagles and Dachshunds. Field trials are competitive events that test a dog's ability to perform the functions for which she was bred. Hunting tests, which are open to retrievers,

---

TITLES AWARDED BY THE AKC

Conformation: Ch. (Champion)

Obedience: CD (Companion Dog); CDX (Companion Dog Excellent); UD (Utility Dog); UDX (Utility Dog Excellent); OTCh. (Obedience Trial Champion)

Field: JH (Junior Hunter); SH (Senior Hunter); MH (Master Hunter); AFCh. (Amateur Field Champion); FCh. (Field Champion)

Lure Coursing: JC (Junior Courser); SC (Senior Courser)

Herding: HT (Herding Tested); PT (Pre-Trial Tested); HS (Herding Started); HI (Herding Intermediate); HX (Herding Excellent); HCh. (Herding Champion)

Tracking: TD (Tracking Dog); TDX (Tracking Dog Excellent)

Agility: NAD (Novice Agility); OAD (Open Agility); ADX (Agility Excellent); MAX (Master Agility)

Earthdog Tests: JE (Junior Earthdog); SE (Senior Earthdog); ME (Master Earthdog)

Canine Good Citizen: CGC

Combination: DC (Dual Champion—Ch. and Fch.); TC (Triple Champion—Ch., Fch., and OTCh.)

spaniels and pointing breeds only, are noncompetitive and are a means of judging the dog's ability as well as that of the handler.

Hunting is a very large and complex part of canine sports, and if you own one of the breeds that hunts, the events are a great treat for your dog and you. He gets to do what he was bred for, and you get to work with him and watch him do it. You'll be proud of and amazed at what your dog can do.

Fortunately, the AKC publishes a series of booklets on these events, which outline the rules and regulations and include a glossary of the sometimes complicated terms. The AKC also publishes newsletters for field trialers and hunting test enthusiasts. The United Kennel Club (UKC) also has informative materials for the hunter and his dog.

Retrievers and other sporting breeds get to do what they're bred to in hunting tests.

HERDING TESTS AND TRIALS

Herding, like hunting, dates back to the first known uses man made of dogs. The interest in herding today is widespread, and if you own a herding breed, you can join in the activity. Herding dogs are tested for their natural skills to keep a flock of ducks, sheep or cattle together. If your dog shows potential, you can start at the testing level, where your dog can earn a title for showing an inherent herding ability. With training you can advance to the trial level, where your dog should be capable of controlling even difficult livestock in diverse situations.

LURE COURSING

The AKC Tests and Trials for Lure Coursing are open to traditional sighthounds—Greyhounds, Whippets,

Borzoi, Salukis, Afghan Hounds, Ibizan Hounds and Scottish Deerhounds—as well as to Basenjis and Rhodesian Ridgebacks. Hounds are judged on overall ability, follow, speed, agility and endurance. This is possibly the most exciting of the trials for spectators, because the speed and agility of the dogs is awesome to watch as they chase the lure (or "course") in heats of two or three dogs at a time.

TRACKING

Tracking is another activity in which almost any dog can compete because every dog that sniffs the ground when taken outdoors is, in fact, tracking. The hard part comes when the rules as to what, when and where the dog tracks are determined by a person, not the dog! Tracking tests cover a large area of fields, woods and roads. The tracks are laid hours before the dogs go to work on them, and include "tricks" like cross-tracks and sharp turns. If you're interested in search-and-rescue work, this is the place to start.

This tracking dog is hot on the trail.

EARTHDOG TESTS FOR SMALL TERRIERS AND DACHSHUNDS

These tests are open to Australian, Bedlington, Border, Cairn, Dandie Dinmont, Smooth and Wire Fox, Lakeland, Norfolk, Norwich, Scottish, Sealyham, Skye, Welsh and West Highland White Terriers as well as Dachshunds. The dogs need no prior training for this terrier sport. There is a qualifying test on the day of the event, so dog and handler learn the rules on the spot. These tests, or "digs," sometimes end with informal races in the late afternoon.

Here are some of the extracurricular obedience and racing activities that are not regulated by the AKC or UKC, but are generally run by clubs or a group of dog fanciers and are often open to all.

Canine Freestyle This activity is something new on the scene and is variously likened to dancing, dressage or ice skating. It is meant to show the athleticism of the dog, but also requires showmanship on the part of the dog's handler. If you and your dog like to ham it up for friends, you might want to look into freestyle.

Lure coursing lets sighthounds do what they do best—run!

Scent Hurdle Racing Scent hurdle racing is purely a fun activity sponsored by obedience clubs with members forming competing teams. The height of the hurdles is based on the size of the shortest dog on the team. On a signal, one team dog is released on each of two side-by-side courses and must clear every hurdle before picking up its own dumbbell from a platform and returning over the jumps to the handler. As each dog returns, the next on that team is sent. Of course, that is what the dogs are supposed to do. When the dogs improvise (going under or around the hurdles, stealing another dog's dumbbell, and so forth), it no doubt frustrates the handlers, but just adds to the fun for everyone else.

Flyball This type of racing is similar, but after negotiating the four hurdles, the dog comes to a flyball box, steps on a lever that releases a tennis ball into the air, catches the ball and returns over the hurdles to the starting point. This game also becomes extremely fun for spectators because the dogs sometimes cheat by catching a ball released by the dog in the next lane. Three titles can be earned—Flyball Dog (F.D.), Flyball Dog Excellent (F.D.X.) and Flyball Dog Champion (Fb.D.Ch.)—all awarded by the North American Flyball Association, Inc.

Dogsledding The name conjures up the Rocky Mountains or the frigid North, but you can find dogsled clubs in such unlikely spots as Maryland, North Carolina and Virginia! Dogsledding is primarily for the Nordic breeds such as the Alaskan Malamutes, Siberian Huskies and Samoyeds, but other breeds can try. There are some practical backyard applications to this sport, too. With parental supervision, almost any strong dog could pull a child's sled.

Coming over the A-frame on an agility course.

These are just some of the many recreational ways you can get to know and understand your multifaceted dog better and have fun doing it.

chapter 10

Your Dog
and your
Family

by Bardi McLennan

Adding a dog automatically increases your family by one, no matter whether you live alone in an apartment or are part of a mother, father and six kids household. The single-person family is fair game for numerous and varied canine misconceptions as to who is dog and who pays the bills, whereas a dog in a houseful of children will consider himself to be just one of the gang, littermates all. One dog and one child may give a dog reason to believe they are both kids or both dogs. Either interpretation requires parental supervision and sometimes speedy intervention.

As soon as one paw goes through the door into your home, Rufus (or Rufina) has to make many adjustments to become a part of your

136

family. Your job is to make him fit in as painlessly as possible. An older dog may have some frame of reference from past experience, but to a 10-week-old puppy, everything is brand new: people, furniture, stairs, when and where people eat, sleep or watch TV, his own place and everyone else's space, smells, sounds, outdoors—everything!

Puppies, and newly acquired dogs of any age, do not need what we think of as "freedom." If you leave a new dog or puppy loose in the house, you will almost certainly return to chaotic destruction and the dog will forever after equate your homecoming with a time of punishment to be dreaded. It is unfair to give your dog what amounts to "freedom to get into trouble." Instead, confine him to a crate for brief periods of your absence (up to three or four hours) and, for the long haul, a workday for example, confine him to one untrashable area with his own toys, a bowl of water and a radio left on (low) in another room.

Lots of pets get along with each other just fine.

For the first few days, when not confined, put Rufus on a long leash tied to your wrist or waist. This umbilical cord method enables the dog to learn all about you from your body language and voice, and to learn by his own actions which things in the house are NO! and which ones are rewarded by "Good dog." Housetraining will be easier with the pup always by your side. Speaking of which, accidents do happen. That goal of "completely housetrained" takes up to a year, or the length of time it takes the pup to mature.

The All-Adult Family

Most dogs in an adults-only household today are likely to be latchkey pets, with no one home all day but the dog. When you return after a tough day on the job, the dog can and should be your relaxation therapy. But going home can instead be a daily frustration.

Separation anxiety is a very common problem for the dog in a working household. It may begin with whines and barks of loneliness, but it will soon escalate into a frenzied destruction derby. That is why it is so important to set aside the time to teach a dog to relax when left alone in his confined area and to understand that he can trust you to return.

Let the dog get used to your work schedule in easy stages. Confine him to one room and go in and out of that room over and over again. Be casual about it. No physical, voice or eye contact. When the pup no longer even notices your comings and goings, leave the house for varying lengths of time, returning to stay home for a few minutes and gradually increasing the time away. This training can take days, but the dog is learning that you haven't left him forever and that he can trust you.

Any time you leave the dog, but especially during this training period, be casual about your departure. No anxiety-building fond farewells. Just "Bye" and go! Remember the "Good dog" when you return to find everything more or less as you left it.

If things are a mess (or even a disaster) when you return, greet the dog, take him outside to eliminate, and then put him in his crate while you clean up. Rant and rave in the shower! *Do not* punish the dog. You were not there when it happened, and the rule is: Only punish as you catch the dog in the act of wrongdoing. Obviously, it makes sense to get your latchkey puppy when you'll have a week or two to spend on these training essentials.

Family weekend activities should include Rufus whenever possible. Depending on the pup's age, now is the time for a long walk in the park, playtime in the backyard, a hike in the woods. Socializing is as important as health care, good food and physical exercise, so visiting Aunt Emma or Uncle Harry and the next-door neighbor's dog or cat is essential to developing an outgoing, friendly temperament in your pet.

If you are a single adult, socializing Rufus at home and away will prevent him from becoming overly protective of you (or just overly attached) and will also prevent such behavioral problems as dominance or fear of strangers.

Babies

Whether already here or on the way, babies figure larger than life in the eyes of a dog. If the dog is there first, let him in on all your baby preparations in the house. When baby arrives, let Rufus sniff any item of clothing that has been on the baby before Junior comes home. Then let Mom greet the dog first before introducing the new family member. Hold the baby down for the dog to see and sniff, but make sure someone's holding the dog on lead in case of any sudden moves. Don't play keep-away or tease the dog with the baby, which only invites undesirable jumping up.

The dog and the baby are "family," and for starters can be treated almost as equals. Things rapidly change, however, especially when baby takes to creeping around on all fours on the dog's turf or, better yet, has yummy pudding all over her face and hands! That's when a lot of things in the dog's and baby's lives become more separate than equal.

Dogs are perfect confidants.

Toddlers make terrible dog owners, but if you can't avoid the combination, use patient discipline (that is, positive teaching rather than punishment), and use time-outs before you run out of patience.

A dog and a baby (or toddler, or an assertive young child) should never be left alone together. Take the dog with you or confine him. With a baby or youngsters in the house, you'll have plenty of use for that wonderful canine safety device called a crate!

Young Children

Any dog in a house with kids will behave pretty much as the kids do, good or bad. But even good dogs and good children can get into trouble when play becomes rowdy and active.

Teach children how to play nicely with a puppy.

Legs bobbing up and down, shrill voices screeching, a ball hurtling overhead, all add up to exuberant frustration for a dog who's just trying to be part of the gang. In a pack of puppies, any legs or toys being chased would be caught by a set of teeth, and all the pups involved would understand that is how the game is played. Kids do not understand this, nor do parents tolerate it. Bring Rufus indoors before you have reason to regret it. This is time-out, not a punishment.

You can explain the situation to the children and tell them they must play quieter games until the puppy learns not to grab them with his mouth. Unfortunately, you can't explain it that easily to the dog. With adult supervision, they will learn how to play together.

Young children love to tease. Sticking their faces or wiggling their hands or fingers in the dog's face is teasing. To another person it might be just annoying, but it is threatening to a dog. There's another difference: We can make the child stop by an explanation, but the only way a dog can stop it is with a warning growl and then with teeth. Teasing is the major cause of children being bitten by their pets. Treat it seriously.

Older Children

The best age for a child to get a first dog is between the ages of 8 and 12. That's when kids are able to accept some real responsibility for their pet. Even so, take the child's vow of "I will never *ever* forget to feed (brush, walk, etc.) the dog" for what it's worth: a child's good intention at that moment. Most kids today have extra lessons, soccer practice, Little League, ballet, and so forth piled on top of school schedules. There will be many times when Mom will have to come to the dog's rescue. "I walked the dog for you so you can set the table for me" is one way to get around a missed appointment without laying on blame or guilt.

Kids in this age group make excellent obedience trainers because they are into the teaching/learning process themselves and they lack the self-consciousness of adults. Attending a dog show is something the whole family can enjoy, and watching Junior Showmanship may catch the eye of the kids. Older children can begin to get involved in many of the recreational activities that were reviewed in the previous chapter. Some of the agility obstacles, for example, can be set up in the backyard as a family project (with an adult making sure all the equipment is safe and secure for the dog).

Older kids are also beginning to look to the future, and may envision themselves as veterinarians or trainers or show dog handlers or writers of the next Lassie best-seller. Dogs are perfect confidants for these dreams. They won't tell a soul.

Other Pets

Introduce all pets tactfully. In a dog/cat situation, hold the dog, not the cat. Let two dogs meet on neutral turf—a stroll in the park or a walk down the street—with both on loose leads to permit all the normal canine ways of saying hello, including routine sniffing, circling, more sniffing, and so on. Small creatures such as hamsters, chinchillas or mice must be kept safe from their natural predators (dogs and cats).

Festive Family Occasions

Parties are great for people, but not necessarily for puppies. Until all the guests have arrived, put the dog in his crate or in a room where he won't be disturbed. A socialized dog can join the fun later as long as he's not underfoot, annoying guests or into the hors d'oeuvres.

There are a few dangers to consider, too. Doors opening and closing can allow a puppy to slip out unnoticed in the confusion, and you'll be organizing a search party instead of playing host or hostess. Party food and buffet service are not for dogs. Let Rufus party in his crate with a nice big dog biscuit.

At Christmas time, not only are tree decorations dangerous and breakable (and perhaps family heirlooms), but extreme caution should be taken with the lights, cords and outlets for the tree lights and any other festive lighting. Occasionally a dog lifts a leg, ignoring the fact that the tree is indoors. To avoid this, use a canine repellent, made for gardens, on the tree. Or keep him out of the tree room unless supervised. And whatever you do, *don't* invite trouble by hanging his toys on the tree!

Car Travel

Before you plan a vacation by car or RV with Rufus, be sure he enjoys car travel. Nothing spoils a holiday quicker than a carsick dog! Work within the dog's comfort level. Get in the car with the dog in his crate or attached to a canine car safety belt and just sit there until he relaxes. That's all. Next time, get in the car, turn on the engine and go nowhere. Just sit. When that is okay, turn on the engine and go around the block. Now you can go for a ride and include a stop where you get out, leaving the dog for a minute or two.

On a warm day, always park in the shade and leave windows open several inches. And return quickly. It only takes 10 minutes for a car to become an overheated steel death trap.

Motel or Pet Motel?

Not all motels or hotels accept pets, but you have a much better choice today than even a few years ago. To find a dog-friendly lodging, look at *On the Road Again With Man's Best Friend*, a series of directories that detail bed and breakfasts, inns, family resorts and other hotels/motels. Some places require a refundable deposit to cover any damage incurred by the dog. More B&Bs accept pets now, but some restrict the size.

If taking Rufus with you is not feasible, check out boarding kennels in your area. Your veterinarian may offer this service, or recommend a kennel or two he or she is familiar with. Go see the facilities for yourself, ask about exercise, diet, housing, and so on. Or, if you'd rather have Rufus stay home, look into bonded petsitters, many of whom will also bring in the mail and water your plants.

Your Dog
and your
Community

by Bardi McLennan

Step outside your home with your dog and you are no longer just family, you are both part of your community. This is when the phrase "responsible pet ownership" takes on serious implications. For starters, it means you pick up after your dog—not just occasionally, but every time your dog eliminates away from home. That means you have joined the Plastic Baggy Brigade! You always have plastic sandwich bags in your pocket and several in the car. It means you teach your kids how to use them, too. If you think this is "yucky," just imagine what

the person (a non-doggy person) who inadvertently steps in the mess thinks!

Your responsibility extends to your neighbors: To their ears (no annoying barking); to their property (their garbage, their lawn, their flower beds, their cat—especially their cat); to their kids (on bikes, at play); to their kids' toys and sports equipment.

There are numerous dog-related laws, ranging from simple dog licensing and leash laws to those holding you liable for any physical injury or property damage done by your dog. These laws are in place to protect everyone in the community, including you and your dog. There are town ordinances and state laws which are by no means the same in all towns or all states. Ignorance of the law won't get you off the hook. The time to find out what the laws are where you live is now.

Be sure your dog's license is current. This is not just a good local ordinance, it can make the difference between finding your lost dog or not. Many states now require proof of rabies vaccination and that the dog has been spayed or neutered before issuing a license. At the same time, keep up the dog's annual immunizations.

Dressing your dog up makes him appealing to strangers.

Never let your dog run loose in the neighborhood. This will not only keep you on the right side of the leash law, it's the outdoor version of the rule about not giving your dog "freedom to get into trouble."

Good Canine Citizen

Sometimes it's hard for a dog's owner to assess whether or not the dog is sufficiently socialized to be accepted by the community at large. Does Rufus or Rufina display good, controlled behavior in public? The AKC's Canine Good Citizen program is available through many dog organizations. If your dog passes the test, the title "CGC" is earned.

The overall purpose is to turn your dog into a good neighbor and to teach you about your responsibility to your community as a dog owner. Here are the ten things your dog must do willingly:

1. Accept a stranger stopping to chat with you.
2. Sit and be petted by a stranger.
3. Allow a stranger to handle him or her as a groomer or veterinarian would.
4. Walk nicely on a loose lead.
5. Walk calmly through a crowd.
6. Sit and down on command, then stay in a sit or down position while you walk away.
7. Come when called.
8. Casually greet another dog.
9. React confidently to distractions.
10. Accept being left alone with someone other than you and not become overly agitated or nervous.

Schools and Dogs

Schools are getting involved with pet ownership on an educational level. It has been proven that children who are kind to animals are humane in their attitude toward other people as adults.

A dog is a child's best friend, and so children are often primary pet owners, if not the primary caregivers. Unfortunately, they are also the ones most often bitten by dogs. This occurs due to a lack of understanding that pets, no matter how sweet, cuddly and loving, are still animals. Schools, along with parents, dog clubs, dog fanciers and the AKC, are working to change all that with video programs for children not only in grade school, but in the nursery school and pre-kindergarten age group. Teaching youngsters how to be responsible dog owners is important community work. When your dog has a CGC, volunteer to take part in an educational classroom event put on by your dog club.

Boy Scout Merit Badge

A Merit Badge for Dog Care can be earned by any Boy
Scout ages 11 to 18. The requirements are not easy, but
amount to a complete course in responsible dog care
and general ownership. Here are just a few of the
things a Scout must do to earn that badge:

Point out ten parts of the dog using the correct
names.

Give a report (signed by parent or guardian) on
your care of the dog (feeding, food used, housing,
exercising, grooming and bathing), plus what has
been done to keep the dog healthy.

Explain the right way to obedience train a dog,
and demonstrate three comments.

Several of the requirements have to do with health
care, including first aid, handling a hurt dog, and
the dangers of home treatment for a serious
ailment.

The final requirement is to know the local laws
and ordinances involving dogs.

There are similar programs for Girl Scouts and 4-H
members.

Local Clubs

Local dog clubs are no longer in existence just to put
on a yearly dog show. Today, they are apt to be the hub
of the community's involvement with pets. Dog clubs
conduct educational forums with big-name speakers,
stage demonstrations of canine talent in a busy mall
and take dogs of various breeds to schools for classroom discussion.

The quickest way to feel accepted as a member in a
club is to volunteer your services! Offer to help with
something—anything—and watch your popularity
(and your interest) grow.

Therapy Dogs

Once your dog has earned that essential CGC and reliably demonstrates a steady, calm temperament, you could look into what therapy dogs are doing in your area.

Therapy dogs go with their owners to visit patients at hospitals or nursing homes, generally remaining on leash but able to coax a pat from a stiffened hand, a smile from a blank face, a few words from sealed lips or a hug from someone in need of love.

Nursing homes cover a wide range of patient care. Some specialize in care of the elderly, some in the treatment of specific illnesses, some in physical therapy. Children's facilities also welcome visits from trained therapy dogs for boosting morale in their pediatric patients. Hospice care for the terminally ill and the at-home care of AIDS patients are other areas where this canine visiting is desperately needed. Therapy dog training comes first.

Your dog can make a differ-ence in lots of lives.

There is a lot more involved than just taking your nice friendly pooch to someone's bedside. Doing therapy dog work involves your own emotional stability as well as that of your dog. But once you have met all the requirements for this work, making the rounds once a week or once a month with your therapy dog is possibly the most rewarding of all community activities.

Disaster Aid

This community service is definitely not for everyone, partly because it is time-consuming. The initial training is rigorous, and there can be no let-up in the continuing workouts, because members are on call 24 hours a day to go wherever they are needed at a moment's notice. But if you think you would like to be able to assist in a disaster, look into search-and-rescue work. The network of search-and-rescue volunteers is worldwide, and all members of the American Rescue Dog Association (ARDA) who are qualified to do this work are volunteers who train and maintain their own dogs.

Physical Aid

Most people are familiar with Seeing Eye dogs, which serve as blind people's eyes, but not with all the other work that dogs are trained to do to assist the disabled. Dogs are also specially trained to pull wheelchairs, carry school books, pick up dropped objects, open and close doors. Some also are ears for the deaf. All these assistance-trained dogs, by the way, are allowed anywhere "No Pet" signs exist (as are therapy dogs when

Making the rounds with your therapy dog can be very rewarding.

properly identified). Getting started in any of this fascinating work requires a background in dog training and canine behavior, but there are also volunteer jobs ranging from answering the phone to cleaning out kennels to providing a foster home for a puppy. You have only to ask.

 part four

Beyond

the

Basics

chapter 12

Recommended Reading

Books

ABOUT HEALTH CARE

Ackerman, Lowell. *Guide to Skin and Haircoat Problems in Dogs*. Loveland, Colo.: Alpine Publications, 1994.

Alderton, David. *The Dog Care Manual*. Hauppauge, N.Y.: Barron's Educational Series, Inc., 1986.

American Kennel Club. *American Kennel Club Dog Care and Training*. New York: Howell Book House, 1991.

Bamberger, Michelle, DVM. *Help! The Quick Guide to First Aid for Your Dog*. New York: Howell Book House, 1995.

Carlson, Delbert, DVM, and James Giffin, MD. *Dog Owner's Home Veterinary Handbook*. New York: Howell Book House, 1992.

DeBitetto, James, DVM, and Sarah Hodgson. *You & Your Puppy*. New York: Howell Book House, 1995.

Humphries, Jim, DVM. *Dr. Jim's Animal Clinic for Dogs*. New York: Howell Book House, 1994.

McGinnis, Terri. *The Well Dog Book*. New York: Random House, 1991.

Pitcairn, Richard and Susan. *Natural Health for Dogs*. Emmaus, Pa.: Rodale Press, 1982.

ABOUT DOG SHOWS

Hall, Lynn. *Dog Showing for Beginners*. New York: Howell Book House, 1994.

Nichols, Virginia Tuck. *How to Show Your Own Dog*. Neptune, N. J.: TFH, 1970.

Vanacore, Connie. *Dog Showing, An Owner's Guide*. New York: Howell Book House, 1990.

ABOUT TRAINING

Ammen, Amy. *Training in No Time*. New York: Howell Book House, 1995.

Baer, Ted. *Communicating With Your Dog*. Hauppauge, N.Y.: Barron's Educational Series, Inc., 1989.

Benjamin, Carol Lea. *Dog Problems*. New York: Howell Book House, 1989.

Benjamin, Carol Lea. *Dog Training for Kids*. New York: Howell Book House, 1988.

Benjamin, Carol Lea. *Mother Knows Best*. New York: Howell Book House, 1985.

Benjamin, Carol Lea. *Surviving Your Dog's Adolescence*. New York: Howell Book House, 1993.

Bohnenkamp, Gwen. *Manners for the Modern Dog*. San Francisco: Perfect Paws, 1990.

Dibra, Bashkim. *Dog Training by Bash*. New York: Dell, 1992.

Dunbar, Ian, PhD, MRCVS. *Dr. Dunbar's Good Little Dog Book*, James & Kenneth Publishers, 2140 Shattuck Ave. #2406, Berkeley, Calif. 94704. (510) 658–8588. Order from the publisher.

Dunbar, Ian, PhD, MRCVS. *How to Teach a New Dog Old Tricks*, James & Kenneth Publishers. Order from the publisher; address above.

Dunbar, Ian, PhD, MRCVS, and Gwen Bohnenkamp. Booklets on *Preventing Aggression; Housetraining; Chewing; Digging; Barking; Socialization; Fearfulness; and Fighting*, James & Kenneth Publishers. Order from the publisher; address above.

Evans, Job Michael. *People, Pooches and Problems*. New York: Howell Book House, 1991.

Kilcommons, Brian and Sarah Wilson. *Good Owners, Great Dogs*. New York: Warner Books, 1992.

McMains, Joel M. *Dog Logic—Companion Obedience*. New York: Howell Book House, 1992.

Rutherford, Clarice and David H. Neil, MRCVS. *How to Raise a Puppy You Can Live With*. Loveland, Colo.: Alpine Publications, 1982.

Volhard, Jack and Melissa Bartlett. *What All Good Dogs Should Know: The Sensible Way to Train*. New York: Howell Book House, 1991.

ABOUT BREEDING

Harris, Beth J. Finder. *Breeding a Litter, The Complete Book of Prenatal and Postnatal Care*. New York: Howell Book House, 1983.

Holst, Phyllis, DVM. *Canine Reproduction*. Loveland, Colo.: Alpine Publications, 1985.

Walkowicz, Chris and Bonnie Wilcox, DVM. *Successful Dog Breeding, The Complete Handbook of Canine Midwifery*. New York: Howell Book House, 1994.

ABOUT ACTIVITIES

American Rescue Dog Association. *Search and Rescue Dogs*. New York: Howell Book House, 1991.

Barwig, Susan and Stewart Hilliard. *Schutzhund*. New York: Howell Book House, 1991.

Beaman, Arthur S. *Lure Coursing*. New York: Howell Book House, 1994.

Daniels, Julie. *Enjoying Dog Agility—From Backyard to Competition*. New York: Doral Publishing, 1990.

Davis, Kathy Diamond. *Therapy Dogs*. New York: Howell Book House, 1992.

Gallup, Davis Anne. *Running With Man's Best Friend*. Loveland, Colo.: Alpine Publications, 1986.

Habgood, Dawn and Robert. *On the Road Again With Man's Best Friend*. New England, Mid-Atlantic, West Coast and Southeast editions. Selective guides to area bed and breakfasts, inns, hotels and resorts that welcome guests and their dogs. New York: Howell Book House, 1995.

Holland, Vergil S. *Herding Dogs*. New York: Howell Book House, 1994.

LaBelle, Charlene G. *Backpacking With Your Dog*. Loveland, Colo.: Alpine Publications, 1993.

Simmons-Moake, Jane. *Agility Training, The Fun Sport for All Dogs*. New York: Howell Book House, 1991.

Spencer, James B. *Hup! Training Flushing Spaniels the American Way*. New York: Howell Book House, 1992.

Spencer, James B. *Point! Training the All-Seasons Birddog*. New York: Howell Book House, 1995.

Tarrant, Bill. *Training the Hunting Retriever*. New York: Howell Book House, 1991.

Volhard, Jack and Wendy. *The Canine Good Citizen*. New York: Howell Book House, 1994.

General Titles

Haggerty, Captain Arthur J. *How to Get Your Pet Into Show Business*. New York: Howell Book House, 1994.

McLennan, Bardi. *Dogs and Kids, Parenting Tips*. New York: Howell Book House, 1993.

Moran, Patti J. *Pet Sitting for Profit, A Complete Manual for Professional Success*. New York: Howell Book House, 1992.

Scalisi, Danny and Libby Moses. *When Rover Just Won't Do, Over 2,000 Suggestions for Naming Your Dog.* New York: Howell Book House, 1993.

Sife, Wallace, PhD. *The Loss of a Pet.* New York: Howell Book House, 1993.

Wrede, Barbara J. *Civilizing Your Puppy.* Hauppauge, N.Y.: Barron's Educational Series, 1992.

Magazines

The AKC GAZETTE, The Official Journal for the Sport of Purebred Dogs. American Kennel Club, 51 Madison Ave., New York, NY.

Bloodlines Journal. United Kennel Club, 100 E. Kilgore Rd., Kalamazoo, MI.

Dog Fancy. Fancy Publications, 3 Burroughs, Irvine, CA 92718

Dog World. Maclean Hunter Publishing Corp., 29 N. Wacker Dr., Chicago, IL 60606.

Videos

"SIRIUS Puppy Training," by Ian Dunbar, PhD, MRCVS. James & Kenneth Publishers, 2140 Shattuck Ave. #2406, Berkeley, CA 94704. Order from the publisher.

"Training the Companion Dog," from Dr. Dunbar's British TV Series, James & Kenneth Publishers. (See address above).

The American Kennel Club produces videos on every breed of dog, as well as on hunting tests, field trials and other areas of interest to purebred dog owners. For more information, write to AKC/Video Fulfillment, 5580 Centerview Dr., Suite 200, Raleigh, NC 27606.

chapter 13

Resources

Breed Clubs

Every breed recognized by the American Kennel Club has a national (parent) club. National clubs are a great source of information on your breed. You can get the name of the secretary of the club by contacting:

The American Kennel Club
51 Madison Avenue
New York, NY 10010
(212) 696-8200

There are also numerous all-breed, individual breed, obedience, hunting and other special-interest dog clubs across the country. The American Kennel Club can provide you with a geographical list of clubs to find ones in your area. Contact them at the above address.

Registry Organizations

Registry organizations register purebred dogs. The American Kennel Club is the oldest and largest in this country, and currently recognizes over 130 breeds. The United Kennel Club registers some breeds the AKC doesn't (including the American Pit Bull Terrier and the Miniature Fox Terrier) as well as many of the same breeds. The others included here are for your reference; the AKC can provide you with a list of foreign registries.

American Kennel Club
51 Madison Avenue
New York, NY 10010

United Kennel Club (UKC)
100 E. Kilgore Road
Kalamazoo, MI 49001-5598

American Dog Breeders Assn.
P.O. Box 1771
Salt Lake City, UT 84110
(Registers American Pit Bull Terriers)

Canadian Kennel Club
89 Skyway Avenue
Etobicoke, Ontario
Canada M9W 6R4

National Stock Dog Registry
P.O. Box 402
Butler, IN 46721
(Registers working stock dogs)

Orthopedic Foundation for Animals (OFA)
2300 E. Nifong Blvd.
Columbia, MO 65201-3856
(Hip registry)

Activity Clubs

Write to these organizations for information on the activities they sponsor.

American Kennel Club
51 Madison Avenue
New York, NY 10010
(Conformation Shows, Obedience Trials, Field Trials and Hunting Tests, Agility, Canine Good

Citizen, Lure Coursing, Herding, Tracking,
Earthdog Tests, Coonhunting.)

United Kennel Club
100 E. Kilgore Road
Kalamazoo, MI 49001-5598
(Conformation Shows, Obedience Trials, Agility,
Hunting for Various Breeds, Terrier Trials and
more.)

North American Flyball Assn.
1342 Jeff St.
Ypsilanti, MI 48198

International Sled Dog Racing Assn.
P.O. Box 446
Norman, ID 83848-0446

North American Working Dog Assn., Inc.
Southeast Kreisgruppe
P.O. Box 833
Brunswick, GA 31521

Trainers

Association of Pet Dog Trainers
P.O. Box 385
Davis, CA 95617
(800) PET–DOGS

American Dog Trainers' Network
161 West 4th St.
New York, NY 10014
(212) 727–7257

**National Association of Dog Obedience
Instructors**
2286 East Steel Rd.
St. Johns, MI 48879

Associations

American Dog Owners Assn.
1654 Columbia Tpk.
Castleton, NY 12033
(Combats anti-dog legislation)

Delta Society
P.O. Box 1080
Renton, WA 98057-1080
(Promotes the human/animal bond through
pet-assisted therapy and other programs)

Dog Writers Assn. of America (DWAA)
Sally Cooper, Secy.
222 Woodchuck Ln.
Harwinton, CT 06791

National Assn. for Search and Rescue (NASAR)
P.O. Box 3709
Fairfax, VA 22038

Therapy Dogs International
6 Hilltop Road
Mendham, NJ 07945